THE METHODS WORK

...if you do!

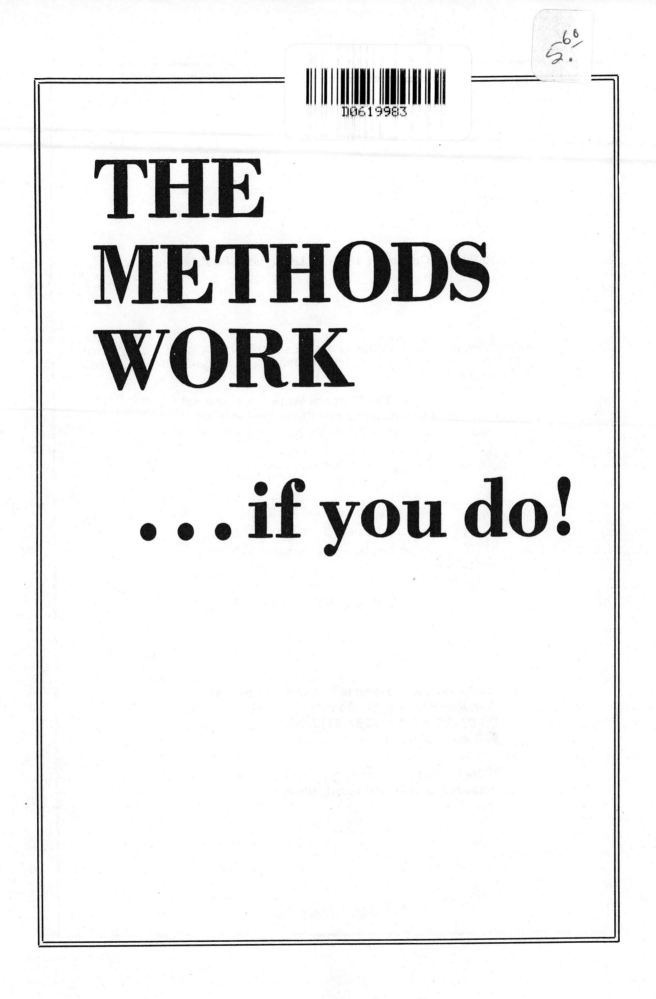

First edition: April, 1978
Second edition: September, 1980
Third edition: December, 1983

ISBN 0-915972-06-9

This workbook is available in bookstores or from Cornucopia Books, 790 Commercial Ave., Coos Bay, OR 97420, tel. (503) 267-4112. Add $1.25 for each $10 worth of books.

Write for free information on trainings, other books, cassettes, posters and record albums.

Drawings by Meg Studer

Dedication

This book is dedicated to all past, present and future students of Living Love through whose sharing, dedication and love these Methods have been brought to life.

The purpose of our
lives is to free ourselves
from all addictive traps,
and thus become One
with the Ocean of
LIVING LOVE

Contents

Introduction

"The Methods Work . . . if you do." The Methods we are referring to are the Living Love Methods as outlined in the **Handbook to Higher Consciousness** by Ken Keyes, Jr. These six Methods help you increase the love, peace and happiness in your life and decrease the separateness and unhappiness.

At the Ken Keyes Center, we live and grow daily with the Living Love Methods. This booklet details our experiences and insights in the uses of the Living Love Methods.

ClearMind Trainings is the training department of the Center founded by Ken Keyes, Jr. to share these Methods. We, the Residents, are individuals from all walks of life, ranging in age from 16 to 61.

We share our lives and our use of the Living Love Methods with people from all over the world in our residential trainings in Coos Bay, Oregon and in weekend workshops in major cities throughout the United States. By using the Methods daily we are opening our hearts and expanding our love, for ourselves and for others. As our minds become clearer and clearer, we sharpen our perceptiveness and increase our energy. We are learning to live our lives more lovingly and more effectively.

In this booklet we share the specific ways in which we use the Living Love Methods. We hope this sharing will help you to gain insight and receive information about the Methods so you may use them effectively in your life.

You will find that as you use the Methods daily you will gain additional insight into each of them. Each and every Method changes as we internalize them. It is a great adventure to discover how the different Methods become more and more effective.

Personalize the Methods—experiment with them—make them yours. Read and reread this booklet; use it as a reference. Use the Methods daily. Practice with them, so that as your skill increases, you can use the Methods immediately when you feel uncomfortable or unhappy.

Love YOURSELF as you grow. Enjoy your life—for that is what it is all about. When you become aware of unhappiness, use the Methods to gain insight, perspective and emotional freedom.

Enjoy your journey to **higher consciousness.** You don't have to wait until you are free of all addictions to enjoy your life. You can start right now.

1

Overview

We all have tried to make our lives "work," or be "effective." We have tried to find love, peace and happiness by attempting to get "enough" from the outside world; by acquiring "enough" money, by getting "enough" education, by finding the "right" job, by attaining prestige, by accumulating lovers, by vowing marriage, by having children.

These all are ways of trying to control our behavior or the behavior of the world around us; trying to be a "good" person, trying to do the "right" things. Even when our lives seemingly were going well, there was still a certain hollowness—the feeling that there must be "more to life."

So, the maneuvering to avoid fear and anger, and the search to find love and peace continued. We read or heard about higher consciousness, spirituality and love. It all sounded good, but our minds questioned: "What do I do when I feel afraid or angry?" "How do I do it?" "How do I obtain and feel love in my life?"

Living Love is the way to DO it! To create love, openness, energy, insight and zest in our lives.

Living Love helps us learn to love ourselves and others just the way we are. Living Love helps us use the times we are feeling unhappy as opportunities to grow, opportunities to learn to emotionally accept what is happening in our lives.

You may be asking, "Is it really possible for me to be accepting emotionally everything that is happening in my life—even the things I don't like?"

Yes, it is. Now, that does not mean you can't put energy into changing things in your life, or that you should stop trying to get what you want.

You can continue to put as much energy as you desire into setting up your world or yourself as you want them to be. With emotional acceptance, we experience a centered, loving place where we can optimally choose to make any changes we want in our lives. Yes, we can learn to experience emotional acceptance and with that we will be able to

Love everyone unconditionally including yourself!

As we take a closer look at our attempts to maneuver life situations we begin to realize that even when we manage to achieve our goal, i.e.that great new job, the "perfect" partner, a wonderful new home, we often still feel something is lacking. This is because we often focus on what only appears will bring us peace and happiness.

In the Living Love System we begin to acknowledge and claim the peace and happiness which is our birthright through a two-fold approach:

1) We focus directly on what would truly bring our peace and happiness (what we call our POSITIVE INTENTION) and open ourselves to achieving that personal experience.

2) We sort through the unskillful and ineffective thought patterns (what we call our addictive programming) that would keep our focus misdirected and striving toward what mistakenly would appear to bring us peace and happiness. To further explore the Living Love System, we begin by defining some basic terminology:

POSITIVE INTENTION: The emotional experience you seek to create through your efforts. The feeling you wish to experience in a given moment.

ADDICTION: An emotion-backed demand, desire, expectation or model that makes you upset or unhappy if it is not satisfied. It may be a demand on yourself, on another person or a situation. Addictions block your experience of your positive intention.

PREFERENCE: A desire that is not backed up with any separating emotions or tensions in the body. It's a preference if you do not create any separating emotions when you do not get what you want. You can put energy into making changes from a preferential space, but you are not attached to the results and remain loving of yourself and others. Preferences are experienced through the fourth, fifth, and sixth centers of consciousness. Preferences allow you to experience your positive intentions.

SUFFERING: The unconscious or conscious experience of any separating feeling in any degree; when suffering is continual, you experience unhappiness.

In the Living Love System, we believe that love, peace and unity is every being's birthright. Indeed, that infinite amounts of love exist in everyone of us, but at times our programming interrupts our experience of that love.

We could compare that love with the ever-present sun. The sun is ALWAYS shining. At times the clouds block some of the sun's rays and we flippantly say "the sun is not shining today". But on further thought - we know it's there shining behind the clouds. Even at midnight the sun is shining.

We have simply "turned the world around" far enough that we exclaim quite certainly "there is no sun!" And again, we realize with further consideration that, indeed the sun is still shining.

In much the same way, love exists in all of us. Often our programming "clouds" our experience of it. And at times we literally turn our emotional world around to the point we are certain we have lost love. But, indeed it is always there.

Living Love offers us ways to clear the clouds away and experience the love which is our birthright. The insight the Living Love system offers us is:

Addictions are the only immediate, practical cause of suffering

Only addictions can interfere with your experience of love.

This means that all our suffering is caused by our addictive programming, not by outside events. When there is no addiction, there is no suffering. When we live with preferential programming, there is no way we can trigger suffering, fear, frustration, anger or jealousy -- or create emotional separation from ourselves or anyone else. With preferential programming we can always feel the love within us. We can always achieve our positive intention.

In the past, when we were aware of unhappiness, sadness, anger or other separating emotions, we felt there was something (an outside event) in our world that was not acting or being as we thought it should. That event wasn't meeting our "models" of how it should be. So, we blamed the outside event for our unhappiness.

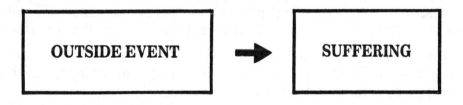

We are now in the process of becoming aware that the outside event is always "filtered" through our programming. It is what we are telling ourselves (our addictive programming) about the outside event that creates the suffering, **not** the outside event.

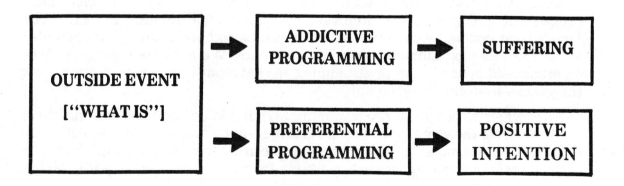

Now, when we use the term "outside events," we are referring to everything that is outside of our conscious-awareness. That includes other people, things, situations; it also includes our bodies, our intelligence, our personality and what we think.

We handled our suffering in the past by attempting to change the outside event. We put time and energy into trying to make the outside event be the way we thought it should be, or to meet our models. Sometimes it worked, depending on how good we were at changing the outside world. But then sometimes it didn't work.

Sometimes, no matter what we do, how we are or what we say, we can't get the outside world to change. And there we are: the outside world won't change, and we think all we can do is to suffer. This is the way many of us have spent most of our lives—suffering when the outside event wasn't the way we thought it should be.

We usually dealt with our suffering and our separating emotions in one of two ways: we either suppressed them by refusing to acknowledge them (automatically we would not even allow our conscious mind to be aware of them); or we expressed them -- our usual way of handling our emotions when we let our conscious mind be aware of them. We expressed them aloud and we acted them out automatically -- robot-like.

Neither of these two methods of dealing with our emotions has been totally successful in our lives. Suppressing our emotions keeps us stuck in our unhappiness. We also create body problems and "greyed out" feelings of unhappiness and low energy. Expressing our feelings makes us feel better than suppressing them, but expression often perpetuates the cycle of separateness and keeps us stuck in experiencing the same emotional patterns again and again and again. And it does nothing at all to free us from the trap of our suffering.

Another way of looking at it is that all of our actions are based on our emotional spaces and what we think. We can change our actions, but that's not going to change our emotional spaces.

We can put energy into suppressing our emotions, but we're still left with what we are thinking. And if that doesn't change, our thinking will continue to create more separating emotions and more expression.

Consequently, the area we want to work with is our thoughts, or our programming, not our actions—not even our emotions. Since our programming is what we operate from, we want to know that we have workable operational programming. Our brain has often been compared to a computer. In fact, in the Living Love system, we refer to the brain as a biocomputer. Just as a computer works from its programming, we work from ours. We are creating our present emotions and actions from programming we have put in our biocomputer over the years—from childhood on up!

Now, when we put in our programming we put it in because it was workable at the time. Over the years, however, we change—our situations change. Although outside events change, our programming doesn't necessarily change. So today at 20, 40 or 60 years of age we are operating from programming we put in at 2, 4 or 6 years of age. And it is no longer workable.

Because we are operating from younger-age programming we find that when something happens (an "outside event") that is not what we want, we suffer. This is opposed to seeing that it's our programming (what we are telling ourselves about this outside event) that causes our unhappiness. We tell ourselves it shouldn't be happening; we want something else; it should be different in order for us to be happy. And that programming is creating the unhappiness in our lives.

What we don't see is that it's the addictions and the addictive programming we have about the way the event "has" to be that is making us upset—**not** the outside event.

With this knowledge we see that "addictions are the **ONLY** cause of suffering and unhappiness in our lives."

All our suffering is caused by our addictive programming. If there is no addictive programming—if there is no addiction—there can be no suffering. If we have preferential programming, there is no way we can trigger suffering (fear, frustration, anger and other separating emotions) or create emotional separation from ourselves or anyone.

The freedom the Living Love system offers us is that we control our addictive programming. We totally control our programming, and it is up to us whether we want to operate on an addictive level or on a preferential level. This also means that we have a new way of dealing with our emotions: we no longer have to suppress them—we no longer have to express them.

With the knowledge that it is our addictive programming that creates our suffering, we can uplevel that addictive programming to preferential programming and consequently deal with the "think out" level. By changing our programming, we also will be changing the resulting emotions.

Simply by operating from preferential programming, as opposed to addictive programming, we no longer will be creating suffering and separation in our lives. This means we retrain our minds to select new programming and give new operating instructions to our biocomputer; this enables us to live more loving, peaceful, effective lives.

We select programming that applies to our situations and to us as adults in this here-and-now world.

In order to reprogram or uplevel those addictions to preferences that are causing our suffering we must first become aware of them. We have to start looking, perhaps for the first time, at the ideas, opinions, judgments and programming that constitute our thoughts.

This will be a new experience for many. Monitoring our thoughts, checking out our thinking and being mindful of our feelings is not something we know how to do automatically. It will take time and practice before we efficiently tune-in to all the programming that goes on in our heads.

The important first step is to acknowledge our thoughts and feelings!

Remember, this is something new. For most of your life your attention has been directed outward toward the outside world. Now you are taking the first steps of directing your attention inward, looking at what's happening inside your own head. It's very similar to the process of learning how to read.

We are very young when we start reading, and we only see certain words and can only make sense out of certain words. That's the way it's going to be as you start looking inward. You are going to see only certain programs. You are going to be aware of only certain addictions.

As you get more and more proficient at seeing how your mind and your programming operate, you will start to put together sentences. You will start to see how much of your addictive programming is connected and how many addictive spaces there are.

It's like a newspaper: first you see the headlines, then you see the story beneath the headlines. Then you get to the second, third and inside pages and then to the want ads, which are in even finer print. That's the process of going inward and exploring our thoughts. So it can be a long process.

In fact, it's a lifetime process! Your job is to be patient with yourself and be gentle with yourself. Realize that it is a journey. All you have to do is enjoy the trip!

We know that we operate totally from our programming. Much of our programming is addictive, some of it is preferential. How do we know when it is addictive and not preferential? The first step is to be aware of what happens with our bodies and our emotions. By simply tuning-in to our emotions and our body sensations, we will learn whether we have an addiction.

You have an addiction:

When you experience tension in your body.

When you experience separating emotions.

When your mind is dominated by how things should be different.

The Living Love Methods give you practical, specific ways to redirect your addictive programming when you are feeling separating emotions. When you become skillful with the Methods, the addictions that trigger suffering don't remain very long, and they are not nearly so emotionally intense. As that happens, your overall enjoyment of life and your love of self and others increase.

The Living Love Methods are tools to help us gain insight and perspective and to help us uplevel our addictions to preferences and alleviate our suffering.

LIVING LOVE METHODS

1. The Twelve Pathways

2. Centers of Consciousness

3. Link the Suffering With the Addiction

4. Catalyst—All Ways Us Living Love

5. Consciousness Focusing

6. The Instant Consciousness Doubler

One of the beauties of the Living Love Methods is they can be used anywhere, any time. You don't have to change your life or any situation in it to use these Methods.

Whenever, wherever you are creating emotional discomfort in your life, you can use these Methods. They work if you do.

In addition to sharing information about pinpointing addictive demands, and the six Methods, this booklet contains detailed information on three dynamic processes that are used to facilitate the use of the Methods.

1. EXPLORATION INSIGHT PROCESS, EIP: A step-by-step process to help us sort through our addictive programming to discover exactly what we are telling ourselves which creates our suffering, to pinpoint specific addictive demand(s), and then use one or more of the Methods to uplevel the demands to preferences.

2. SHARING OF SPACE, SOS: Sharing our addictive thoughts and emotions is an integral part of growing. This process is designed to help us consciously share our addictive spaces with other persons involved. It is a form for sharing exactly what we are feeling while taking responsibility for creating that emotional experience. It adds more light and less heat when communicating about "touchy" things.

3. THE CHOICE PROCESS: A simple process to help you open up to choices and alternatives in your life. As you find creative new ways to achieve your positive intentions, you take a giant step toward the experience of joy and peace you seek.

HOW TO BENEFIT FROM THE LIVING LOVE SYSTEM

When You Become Aware of Separating Emotions
(fear, frustration, anger, jealousy, etc.)

YOU CAN CHOOSE TO

Ignore it, * don't acknowledge it.	**Acknowledge it, **** simply continue to feel it, or express the feeling ***	**Transcend it ****** by changing the programming that creates that experience.
Repress it, * pretend it isn't there.		

* These two choices are NOT RECOMMENDED. They can lead to severe physical and psychological complications.

** This choice is difficult to maintain and often slowly fades into repression.

*** Expression often perpetuates the cycle of separateness.

**** This choice generally is the most successful, life-giving and lasting approach.

TO TRANSCEND ADDICTIVE PROGRAMMING USE THE METHODS

You may enhance your use of the Methods with one
of the following optional processes.

EIP see page 57	CHOICE PROCESS see page 80	Pinpoint Addictive Demand Then Identify Your Positive Intention. see pages 17-22	Do an S.O.S. see page 82

Whether or not you use one of these processes, remember to

USE THE METHODS!

The accompanying diagram outlines the choices available to you when you are experiencing separating emotions. As you see, there are various ways of using the Living Love Methods and processes. A choice is always open to you. Of course, you don't have to use the Methods, either! You may choose either to express your feelings or even to repress them—just be aware of what that creates in your life.

Whatever you choose offers you an opportunity for growth. You don't have to force yourself, and you don't have to be unhappy. You can choose to use the Living Love Methods to uplevel your addictive programming to preferential programming and enjoy your positive intentions.

Be gentle with yourself. Honor your addictions. There is absolutely nothing wrong with addictions. All addictions are messages--they are gifts. They are simply flags that are telling you, "Hey! At this point in your life you are letting past programming interfere with your experience of love!"

You can always change the programming. You do have a choice. So the game is wanting to find more addictions. You want to find all the addictions you can. You don't want to get by with just a few.

Let yourself be exactly where you are, experiencing whatever you are feeling. There's no need to pretend that you do not have separating emotions, or any addictions, or that you are "always loving." Be yourself! Being you gives everyone around you permission to feel and share separating emotions and addictions. It also helps you see which addictions you need to explore in order to grow. It doesn't help you grow when you use your energy to get down on yourself. Let your path unfold in its own way, at its own rate. Use the **Handbook to Higher Consciousness, How to Enjoy Your Life in Spite of It All** and this **Methods Booklet** to help guide you in your journey.

Be gentle with yourself

You'll hear us saying very often, "BE GENTLE WITH YOURSELF." That, perhaps, is the key. Love and accept yourself every step of the way exactly where you are. Realize that at each moment your addiction, this space, these feelings, are perfect for your growth. See that in every moment life is offering you exactly what you need: exactly what you need to be happy and enjoy it all, or exactly what you need to work through the addictive spaces to see the beauty in each moment.

So, be gentle with yourself. We don't expect a third grader to be able to do the problems of a college math major. We don't expect a 10-year-old to act like a 25-year-old. And you don't need to expect yourself to be any different from what you are. Love yourself at each moment and honor the lesson each moment brings.

As you experiment and practice, you will automatically sense which choice will work best for you at any particular time. And if one Method does not work on a particular addictive demand, try another and then another. Sometimes you may have to use all of them . . . several times. We will give you this guarantee:

The Methods Work...if you do!

Pinpointing Addictive Demands

The Living Love Methods provide us with insight into how we are creating our experience of life. They open us to see the alternatives that have always been available to us for consciously choosing the experience we prefer.

When you are unhappy (experiencing separating emotions), you have one or more addictions at play.

Addictions are the only cause of suffering

Many times your programming tells you you must hang on to your addictive demand. Yet, in order to free yourself from the suffering, you must be willing to let go of your addictive demand or uplevel it to a preference. Before this choice can be made, you need to know specifically what you are demanding in each situation. Then you will have all of the information necessary to decide which you want more: (1) freedom from suffering or (2) satisfying your addictive demand.

To pinpoint your specific addictive demand, first get in touch with what you are feeling. Scan your body for pain, tension or other uncomfortable physical sensations. Our bodies are excellent barometers of our emotional condition. They may be the first indication to us that something is bothering us. From this vantage point it is easier to track down the specific emotions to tune you in to your feelings. Your skill in pinpointing specific emotions and differentiating one from another will increase with practice.

When you are in touch with your specific emotions, listen to what your programming is telling you that you have to have to be happy. There may be more than one thing that you want to be different. Sort through your demands until you come to the one central demand that you want satisfied in the particular situation. Avoid vague, general demands, such as "I want to be happy," "I want to be loved," "I want to be treated fairly," etc.

Be specific!

In the precise moment you triggered the separating emotions, what did you want to change? When another person is involved, use his/her name. Don't be surprised if you find that your specific demands are petty, irrational or indefensible. Remember, this is only your programming; it is not who you really are. Allow yourself to have the full range of programming you have accumulated since childhood. Limiting yourself to the acknowledgment of only "good," "adult" or "socially acceptable" addictions will only block you in your growth. Follow the sixth Pathway and see how you are lovable just the way you are, even with addictions. You'll find your love and compassion for others increasing as you do.

When you have pinpointed your addiction, put it in the following form:

I create the experience of
(list your separating emotions)
_____

because I choose to demand
(what you want)
_____

This form is designed to reinforce our willingness to take responsibility for our experience. It helps us to avoid blaming the people and situations around us for our suffering. See how you are actually choosing your present experience and that you are the only one who can choose to change that experience.

Here is a reference list of questions that you can ask yourself to help pinpoint your addictive demand:

—What do I really want in this situation? What don't I want?

—What do I want the most?

—What is it I feel I need in order to be happy?

—What would I like to be different in this situation?

—How do I want things to be?

—What's bothering me the most in this situation?

—What would I ask a magic genie for in this situation?

—What would I complain about to my best friend?

—How do I think things should be or shouldn't be?

—How do I want the people around me to be? How do I want me to be?

—How should I be treated?

—What am I avoiding?

—What is the threat in this situation?

—What's the worst thing that could happen?

Remember, addictions are not right or wrong, fair or unfair, sensible or silly, logical or illogical. Your addiction is simply what you want in any particular situation. Stay tuned-in to your emotions and what you really feel. Be honest about what you want, be specific, avoid intellectualizing your addictive demands away.

18

Be specific!

It is more difficult to use the Methods effectively when the demand is vague, general or intellectual; or contains judgmental rather than descriptive terms. As you pinpoint your demand, define your terms and name the names of the people involved. See the difference in the following examples:

General demand: "I create the experience of fear because I choose to demand love".

Specific demand: "I create the experience of fear because I choose to demand Carole say, 'I love you'."

General demand: "I create the experience of anger because I choose to demand she not be so stupid."

Specific demand: "I create the experience of anger because I choose to demand Betty not forget our money when we go to the grocery store."

We've been functioning from addictive programming for years and ego is not ready to immediately give up whole general areas of addictive programming at once. Working on one specific demand at a time makes using the Methods faster and easier, and that makes inner work much simpler.

Many times it's easy to get impatient and want to reprogram those whole general areas of addictions at once. Many people experience separating emotions because they don't like to be criticized. The general demand would be

"I create the experience of anger because I choose to demand that people not criticize."

If you try to work on that general demand, you will find that your ego and rational mind don't want to accept the reprogramming

"I can be happy when people criticize me."

When you make the demand specific,

"I create the experience of anger because I choose to demand that Jerry not say my presentation was weak,"

you give your ego and rational mind a little breathing space. Your ego and rational mind can accept

"I can be happy when Jerry says my presentation is weak,"

much easier than the general phrase

"I can be happy when people criticize me."

You want to make it as easy as possible for your ego and rational mind to accept the new programming you want in your life. Working on one specific demand is the optimal way to achieve that. It's also the quickest way to reprogram your general addictive areas.

It works like a platform that is supported by pillars. The platform is your general addictive demand, the pillars are your specific demands supporting the general area. If you try to knock the platform over by jumping up and down on top of it, you don't have much success. The platform is too solid. But by working on the specific pillars, knocking them out one at a time, you reach the point where the platform is first shaky and then falls. There are simply not enough pillars left to support the platform.

It works the same way with your addictions. Once you have reprogrammed your specific demand, you then expand that insight into other areas of programming. Your automatic emotional reactions become less intense or even nonexistent. You let go of each similar addiction faster and faster. Your general demand will soon disappear because the individual specific demands that supported it have been reprogrammed.

If you are still having trouble connecting with a specific demand, remember that you can use the Exploration Insight Process as a tool to help you explore your programming. If all attempts fail and you just can't seem to pinpoint your demand, that's OK too. Because you just:

USE ONE OR MORE
LIVING LOVE METHODS

Use one of the Methods that is effective even if you haven't pinpointed your demand, such as the Pathways, Centers of Consciousness, or the Catalyst.

3

Positive Intentions

With everyone and everything we relate to, we have a positive intention: generally to love and/or to be loved. Also within each of these relationships we usually experience addictions. It is helpful to notice that behind every addiction is a POSITIVE INTENTION. (Behind the clouds the sun is always shining!)

Your positive intention is the **internal experience** that you really want in a particular situation, behind the surface desire. It is a general feeling that you want to have: for instance, a positive intention to feel loved, to feel competent, to feel strong.

Your addiction is an unskillful way that you go about trying to achieve your positive intention. So, for example, you might addictively demand that your lover want to go to the movies with you tonight and you might feel angry because s/he doesn't want to go. And behind that addiction, what you really want (your positive intention) is to feel close to that person!

HOW TO IDENTIFY YOUR POSITIVE INTENTION

When you have an addiction, here are some questions you can ask yourself to help you find your positive intention:

What emotional experience did you think you could create by getting what you wanted?

What is the feeling you are **really** after?

Imagine that you have gotten your demand fulfilled or satisfied. How would you be feeling?

What feeling are you really looking for by demanding that?

What feeling do you really want behind that addiction?

What feeling were you hoping to get by demanding that?

As you identify the desired experience it's important to:

1. State it in the positive: what you want rather than what you don't want.

2. Make sure that it can be initiated and maintained by you.

Since your control over anything other than your internal experience is limited, the positive intention must relate to a desired feeling within you.

You are totally and solely responsible for your own emotional experience, so you can always achieve your positive intentions - whether or not your demands are met!

An effective way to assure you meet the two criteria of the positive intention is to use the following form:

"My positive intention is to feel (creative)," or "My positive intention is to see myself as (creative)."

Notice that you wouldn't have a positive intention to **be** creative -- your positive intention is an internal experience.

Here's a list of some POSSIBLE POSITIVE INTENTIONS:

acceptable	alive	beautiful	competent
accepted	appreciated	calm	complete
accepting	athletic	capable	confident
acknowledged	attractive	comfortable	dependable

Bringing together the addictive demand and positive intention helps us recognize more clearly our unskillful attempts at happiness and focus clearly on what we **most** want. This is how we bring it together.

I create the experience of frustration, anger, resentment, disappointment because I choose to demand that Sally and Judy clean up their room. My positive intention is to feel comfortable in my home, to feel peaceful.

I create the experience of hurt because I choose to demand that Sam say I look good in my new dress. My positive intention is to feel attractive.

Identifying your positive intention helps to open up alternative ways to achieve that intention. It helps to remind you to love yourself with that addiction. You can more clearly see how your addictions are just ineffective, unskillful attempts to achieve what you really want (behind the demand). Once you have identified the positive intention, you can approach it directly.

Behind every action, thought, or demand there is always a beneficial positive intention.

4

The Twelve Pathways
(Method No. 1)

> "The Twelve Pathways are a modern, practical condensation of thousands of years of accumulated wisdom. They give you a minute-to-minute guide for operating your consciousness while you interact with the world around you."
>
> [*Handbook to Higher Consciousness, page 12*]

The Twelve Pathways can serve as a guide to bring your true positive intention into a present moment experience. They remind us that our addictive programming actually interferes with our experience of Love and Unity.

The Twelve Pathways as a Method

The Pathways are an excellent Method to use whether or not you have pinpointed your demand. As with all the Methods, the Pathways work best if used immediately. The moment you feel any separating emotion:

Say All Twelve Pathways, Slowly and Meditatively

They will rechannel your thought pattern from the addictive programming to loving and practical reprogramming. They allow insights to come through without engaging your rational mind. Our egos want to make our inner work much more difficult than it actually is. Just do this simple practice. You will be amazed at the results.

There is another way to use the Pathways when you feel uptight and haven't pinpointed your addictive demand or positive intention:

Choose one or more of the Pathways that apply in that situation and say them over and over.

There is no right or wrong Pathway. Choose the one that feels right to you in that particular situation.

Of course, you can use the Pathways when you have pinpointed your addictive demand and positive intention:

State your positive intention alternately with each of the Twelve Pathways.

Experience how each of the Twelve Pathways can have different insights to offer in any and all situations.

The Twelve

Freeing Myself

1 I am freeing myself from security, sensation and power addictions that make me try to forcefully control situations in my life, and thus destroy my serenity and keep me from loving myself and others.

2 I am discovering how my consciousness-dominating addictions create my illusory version of the changing world of people and situations around me.

3 I welcome the opportunity [even if painful] that my minute-to-minute experience offers me to become aware of the addictions I must reprogram to be liberated from my robot-like emotional patterns.

Being Here and Now

4 I always remember that I have everything I need to enjoy my here and now—unless I am letting my consciousness be dominated by demands and expectations based on the dead past or the imagined future.

5 I take full responsibility here and now for everything I experience, for it is my own programming that creates my actions and also influences the reactions of people around me.

6 I accept myself completely here and now and consciously experience everything I feel, think, say and do [including my emotion-backed addictions] as a necessary part of my growth into higher consciousness.

Pathways

Interacting With Others

7 I open myself genuinely to all people by being willing to fully communicate my deepest feelings, since hiding in any degree keeps me stuck in my illusion of separateness from other people.

8 I feel with loving compassion the problems of others without getting caught up emotionally in their predicaments that are offering them messages they need for their growth.

9 I act freely when I am tuned-in, centered and loving, but if possible I avoid acting when I am emotionally upset and depriving myself of the wisdom that flows from love and expanded consciousness.

Discovering my Conscious-awareness

10 I am continually calming the restless scanning of my rational mind in order to perceive the finer energies that enable me to unitively merge with everything around me.

11 I am constantly aware of which of the Seven Centers of Consciousness I am using, and I feel my energy, perceptiveness, love and inner peace growing as I open all of the Centers of Consciousness.

12 I am perceiving everyone, including myself, as an awakening being who is here to claim his or her birthright to the higher consciousness planes of unconditional love and oneness.

You also can:

State your positive intention alternately with one or more Pathways that apply to your specific situation.

Make the connection in your mind so the next time that demand is triggered, the Pathway will come to mind immediately.

All of these ways of using the Pathways may be used in Step E of an EIP.

In order to maximally use the Twelve Pathways, you **must memorize them word perfectly.** When we experience separating emotions, our egos tend to forget the Pathways entirely, or to leave out important words or phrases. Memorizing them word perfectly is the only way they are available to use when we need them. Once we memorize the Pathways, we will begin to experience them on deeper and deeper levels of consciousness.

TIPS FOR MEMORIZING

—Memorize them one at a time (perhaps one a day, one a week or one a month).

—Work with someone else.

—Put copies around your house so that you see and read the Pathways frequently: on the refrigerator, in the bathroom, by the phone, etc.

—Memorize them one word or phrase at a time: "I," "I am," "I am freeing," "I am freeing myself," etc.

—Put them on tape and listen to them before you go to sleep, when you get up in the morning, and several times a day.*

—Put them to music.

—Put them in your pocket or around your wrist.

—Draw a picture of each Pathway.

—Use main words as cues, "I am freeing . . . addictions." "I am discovering . . . illusions."

—Read them out loud before going to sleep, upon waking in the morning and several times a day.

Be patient
━━━━━━━━━━━━━━━━━━━━━━━

If you find yourself creating frustration as you memorize the Pathways, and you are telling yourself you "can't memorize them," acknowledge that as addictive programming. Use the Methods to uplevel the addictions to preferences. Memorizing the Pathways reinforces your determination to eliminate separation and suffering from your life. You are showing determination to become master of your life.

The Twelve Pathways, a 60-minute tape cassette, featuring several repetitions of the Pathways, is available for $6 plus $1.25 postage from Living Love Publications.

5

Centers of Consciousness
(Method No. 2)

"The seven Centers of Consciousness 'act as filters that generate your particular private experience of the here and now in your life.' "

[*Handbook to Higher Consciousness, page 44*]

EVERY MOMENT-TO-MOMENT SITUATION CAN BE VIEWED FROM EACH OF THE CENTERS OF CONSCIOUSNESS

Your emotional experience of any situation depends on the programming filter you use to interpret that situation in your life. When you use programming from the security, sensation and power centers of consciousness, your attention and energy are preoccupied (distorted to varying degrees) with trying to find "enough" security, "enough" sensation and "enough" power.

> ## The Centers of Consciousness
> 1. **Security**
> 2. **Sensation**
> 3. **Power**
> 4. **Love**
> 5. **Cornucopia**
> 6. **Conscious-awareness**
> 7. **Cosmic Consciousness**

These addictive filters limit your energy, distort your perceptions, trigger separating emotions and create separateness in your life. When you use the programming from the love, cornucopia or conscious-awareness centers, you experience your life with love and emotional acceptance of whatever is happening. You are able to preferentially direct your energy toward changes without being attached to the results. You are able to open yourself to claiming your positive intention as an emotional reality.

REMEMBER: You determine your center[s] of consciousness by what you feel and the programming that is triggered. Your center of consciousness is NOT determined by what you do or what is happening.

Following is an outline of the Centers of Consciousness with the emotions and typical programming associated with each center. The programming relates to the following situation: Harry doesn't show up for a date.

1. Security—Wanting emotional or physical security.

A. Usual emotions:

fear	sadness	guilt	envy
anxiety	terror	grief	helplessness
nervousness	horror	confusion	doubt
embarrassment	panic	worry	
hurt	disappointment	jealousy	despair

B. Some typical programming and addictive demands relating to the situation, Harry doesn't show up for a date, may be:

"I'm afraid Harry doesn't care for me any more. I just know that people at school will think I'm no fun to be with. No one will ask me out ever again. Maybe I'm too fat. Maybe he went out with Helen instead."

2. Sensation—Wanting sensations. This includes all sensations a person could demand: food, sex, physical comfort, music, lack of pain, participation in a sport, the right temperature, touching.

A. Usual emotions:

frustration	disgust	disappointment
boredom	jealousy	grief

B. Typical programming and addictive demands relating to the situation, Harry doesn't show up for a date, may be:

"I feel disappointed and frustrated because I won't get to have sex with Harry tonight. Also, I won't get to have that delicious dinner at that restaurant. I'm bored because now there is nothing for me to do. I'll watch television. Hummm, nothing good on. Maybe I'll go get some ice cream or make some popcorn. I'll sit on that neat new chair. Oh shucks, the cat peed on it and it smells disgusting."

3. Power—Wanting either to control, manipulate, or to protect and maintain a particular image, role or territory.

A. Usual emotions:

anger	hostility	disdain
irritation	indignation	resentment
annoyance	rage	hate
frustration	jealousy	fury
impatience		

B. Typical programming:

"How dare he treat me that way. I'm so angry I could scream. I really resent him. I don't want to date him anyway. Damn, I passed up a date with John to go out with Harry. I'll show him. Who does he think he is, anyway? He's got his nerve, not even calling me."

4. Love—The unconditional emotional acceptance of everyone and everything around us. You still have your preferences. You view people, yourself and situations not in terms of how they meet your addictive needs but in terms of, "Well, that's what is—here and now." You are emotionally accepting the situation, even when you put energy into changing it.

A. Usual emotions:

joy	love	happiness
peace	contentment	

B. Typical programming:

"Hummm, Harry's not here. I don't want to create any illusions about what's happening with him. I could call or go over to see him, or I think I'll put my energy into creating a beautiful time with me. I've wanted some time for myself. I feel peaceful and still feel love for Harry."

5. Cornucopia—You experience your life as one beautiful or "miraculous" happening after another. You have more than you need to be happy. Everything that happens is perfect for you to enjoy or for you to honor and experience the opportunity to get free of an addiction.

A. Usual emotions:

joy	love	happiness
peace	contentment	satisfaction
bliss		appreciation

B. Typical programming:

"I now get to enjoy the time by myself. I can put on a new phonograph record. I've been wanting some time to myself and now I've got it and can enjoy being with me. I can write a letter to my friend Sylvia and tell her how much I love her. I can appreciate the opportunity to work on my addiction to being with Harry and to having him be here when he says he will."

6. Conscious-awareness—Nonjudgmental awareness of yourself and others including your drama. It's a "third" person view of your life, as if you were an actor in a movie. You see everyone in the drama trying to love and be loved.

A. Usual emotions:

joy	contentment	gratitude
peace	happiness	serenity
love	satisfaction	

B. Typical programming:

"There she is, playing the part of the hurt girl friend, feeling lonely and sad, as though Harry has to be here for her to feel worthwhile and enough. She's really into the security role and then into the power role—making him wrong and holding on to that. There is the 'Harry-not-showing-up' drama unfolding perfectly."

Or "There she is, creating a beautiful adventure for herself. Harry doesn't come, and she flows with that and enjoys her evening."

7. Cosmic Consciousness—Being one with everything.

Centers of Consciousness as a Method

Centers of Consciousness, as a Method, helps you gain perspective and distance from your addictive programming. It helps you realize how you create your experiences by what you are telling yourself. It helps you see that you choose your experience. You can use your imagination to change your experience by moving your energy to a different center. It helps you learn to uplevel your addictions to preferences. You do not need to know your addictive demand to use this Method. However, at times, your demand could be helpful in pinpointing your center of consciousness. One way to use Centers of Consciousness is simply:

BE AWARE OF WHICH CENTER[S] YOU
ARE USING TO CREATE YOUR EXPERIENCE

Do this whenever you feel separating emotions. Practice! Then you can easily pinpoint what center you are in. Also, stop yourself occasionally during the day and check yourself out to see what center you are in.

By being aware of your center of consciousness, you will be able to move from center to center more easily. Sometimes that awareness gives you enough perspective to create a totally new experience. As you continue to use this method, you become conscious of the patterns of your security, sensation and power dramas.

Remember, you pinpoint your center of consciousness by the emotions you are feeling and/or the thoughts and programming in your head, not by your actions.

Another way to use Centers of Consciousness as a Method:

IMAGINE A SCENE FROM SEVERAL DIFFERENT CENTERS

Use your imagination to see the different ways you can create your experience of a situation. Choose a situation, then change the center of consciousness you use to experience that scene.

First, imagine the scene through the security center. Experience how you would feel, the thought you would be thinking, how others involved would seem. Imagine how your body sensations would be.

Next go to the sensation center and again experience the scene played through that center. Notice the changes in your body, your emotions, your thoughts.

Try the power center next. The same scene played through the power center is totally different. Experience all the changes when you play the scene from this center.

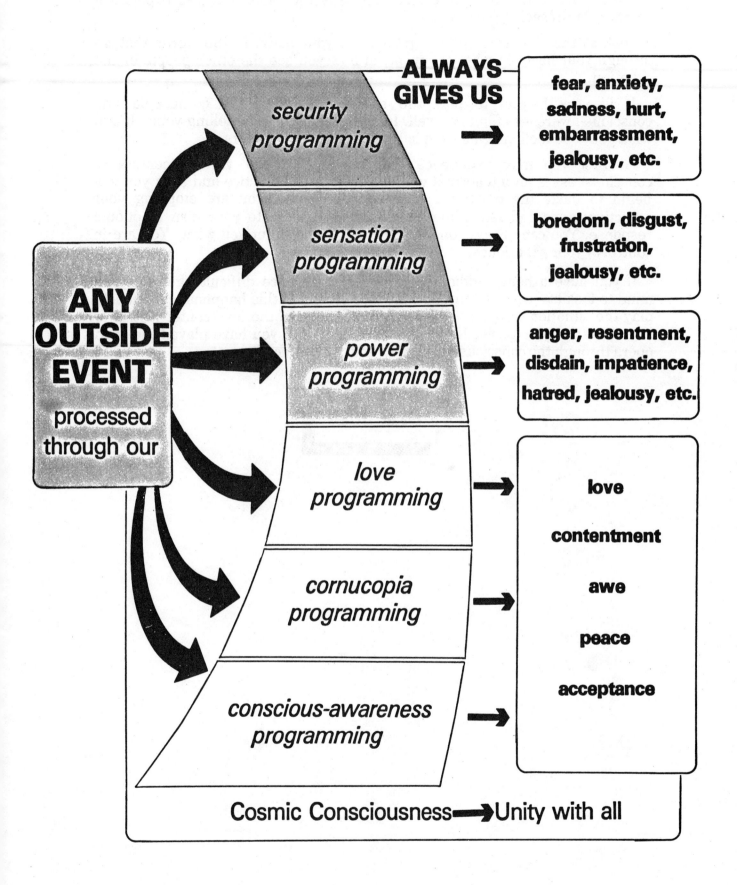

Then move to the love center. The scene is the same, but you experience another way of seeing the drama.

Look at the change in your emotions, in your body, in the words that go through your head, in what you want, in how you see the other people or the situation.

It is very helpful to play the situation through the cornucopia and conscious-awareness filters as well. Imagine what you'd be telling yourself and what you'd be feeling if you were in the fifth and sixth centers.

At first you may experience that moving through various centers of consciousness is an intellectual game. Continue the practice and soon you will begin to make the emotional connections, even if you are stopping your addictive tapes and reminding yourself that you create your own emotional response. You can always consciously choose what filter you want. You are in control of your experience.

If you have a heavy addiction, you may experience difficulty getting your mind to look at "what is" through the love center. If this happens, consciously play the situation through the other centers and use the love center last. The love center may be easier for your mind to use after you have played the soap opera through the conscious-awareness and the cornucopia centers.

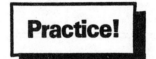

Practice!

6

Link the Suffering With the Addiction
(Method No. 3)

"The key to the Third Method is to consciously connect all of the suffering in your life with the addictive, emotion-backed models and expectations that you keep telling yourself you must have to be happy."

[*Handbook to Higher Consciousness, page 86*]

To Link the Suffering With the Addiction means you get the intellectual and emotional insight, in each specific situation, that it is your addictive demand that is causing your suffering. With this Method you become aware of the way in which it is your addiction—not the outside event—which keeps you on a yo-yo of pleasure and pain. This Method is your emotional realization that

> # Addictions are the only immediate, practical cause of suffering

Remember, when you experience separating emotions, it is the result of one or more addictive demands that are not being satisfied. You free yourself from suffering when your specific addictive demands are handled. Any other remedy is temporary in nature and only delays the inevitable realization that all suffering stems from addictions.

We have all programmed ourselves to seek relief from suffering by changing ourselves or the people and situations in our lives. Our biocomputers will tend to continue functioning in this preprogrammed pattern even though we tell ourselves we want to start linking our suffering to our addictions. To experience the benefit of this Method on the deeper levels of emotional experience, we must learn to consciously overcome our own outmoded mental habits.

To gain an emotional connection between suffering and addiction, two steps are essential:

[1] **Explore your suffering:** Become increasingly aware of the full extent of suffering and separation you experience whenever your addiction is triggered. Avoid qualifying or "explaining away" any part of the psychological, emotional and physical pain you create by holding on to your addictive demand.

[2] **Pinpoint your addiction:** Know specifically what you are demanding in the particular situation. What one thing must you have before you will release your suffering? Acknowledge to yourself that the way life is (or "what is") in that moment is not the cause of your suffering. See that your resistance to the "what is" in your life creates your suffering.

When these steps are successfully completed, your suffering stops. Your ability to flow your energy into constructive action is actually increased. And just because you have given up your suffering does not necessarily mean that you will change your opinion about "what is." You may still not like it and you could still put all of your energy into changing "what is." The only difference is that you do not suffer when things do not go the way you prefer.

Linking the Suffering With the Addiction can take place in a matter of seconds or it may take months, depending upon

[1] YOUR DETERMINATION TO BE FREE OF SUFFERING

[2] YOUR WILLINGNESS TO LET GO OF YOUR ADDICTIVE DEMAND

We often experience ourselves "hanging on" to our addiction even though we tell ourselves we wish to be free of suffering. This occurs as the result of our old mental patterns of blaming the outside world for our own painful predicaments. Our biocomputers have been programmed to suppress our experience of suffering and to cloak our addictions under a smoke screen of rationalizations and blame.

We can rapidly cut holes in this smoke screen by becoming aware of the many clever defense mechanisms our minds continually devise to perpetuate the illusion that "the world is doing it to us." We call these defense mechanisms "payoffs" because they are the tempting rewards sought by the separate-self. Typical payoffs include "being right," "feeling superior," and "avoiding taking responsibility for what I do, say or feel." By increasing our awareness of our payoffs we erode their ability to keep us stuck in our illusion of separateness.

When you find yourself seduced by the payoffs into a perpetuation of separateness and suffering, love yourself. You will have plenty of future opportunities to Link the Suffering With the Addiction. Just keep an objective perspective on the illusory nature of the payoffs. Remember, when payoffs determine your choice:

What you perpetuate is:	**What you forgo is:**
[1] Isolation	[1] Involvement
[2] Crystallized opinions	[2] Wisdom
[3] Suffering	[3] Love

It can feel good, at least temporarily, to be right, to feel superior, to experience the intensity of our anger, to play "poor me," to avoid responsibility for our experiences, to commiserate with sympathizers, etc. But the price we pay in lost peace, insight and love is always far greater.

The following is a graphical representation of this four-step process of Linking the Suffering With the Addiction.

1. **Explore your suffering** (Look at all the ways your enjoyment of life is being ripped off.)

2. **Pinpoint your addictive demand** (What primary thing has to be different for you to stop suffering?)

I create the experience of _____

because I choose to demand_____

_____

"**What is**" (This is what you don't want to emotionally accept. Use the same words as in your addictive demand.)

Restate your addictive demand: "I am emotionally resisting_____

_____."

Realize that in this here-and-now moment "what is" cannot be changed by you in any way. There is absolutely nothing you can do about it right here and now. See that without this addictive demand others are able to enjoy or accept the above "what is." Your suffering is caused by your addictive demand, not by "what is."

3. **The choice is yours**

UPLEVEL TO A PREFERENCE
1. Suffering stops
2. You can more skillfully achieve your positive intention
3. You can maintain your positive intention
4. You can still dislike "what is"
5. You can continue to try to change "what is"

HOLD ON TO THE ADDICTION
1. Suffering continues
2. "What is" often remains the same
3. It interferes with achieving your positive intention

4. **When you discover yourself holding on to the addiction, be aware of the payoffs determining your choice.**

What you perpetuate is:
1. Isolation
2. Crystallized opinions
3. Suffering

What you forgo is:
1. Involvement
2. Wisdom
3. Love

EXPLORE YOUR SUFFERING
[Really get into the rip-offs]

—Look at the pattern of suffering this demand has caused in your life.

—See the past, present and future suffering.

—See how you have suffered in different situations with different people because your programming hasn't changed. You will get in touch with that demand again and again.

—Imagine you have changed a situation to the way you want it to be, and see the suffering you unnecessarily caused yourself. The addiction often prevents you from actually changing what you want to change.

Or you can look at the rip-offs that addiction causes. How many apply in your specific situation?

Look at your	Possible suffering and/ or rip-offs	As a preference you could experience
Body reactions—	Tenseness, tightness, clumsiness, weakness, queasiness; sometimes pain and illness.	Relaxed body.
Emotions—	Separating: fear, frustration, anger, etc.	Love, joy, harmony, etc.
Attitude toward self and other people—	Inability to feel love for others; limited or no love; critical; judgmental.	Love and closeness; emotional acceptance of self and others.
Response toward what is happening in your life—	Distorted perceptions; inability to appreciate the beauty that is available; lots of illusions.	Enjoyment of your here and now; greater awareness of all the beauty that is available in any one moment.
Energy—	Low energy; lots of energy wasted by feeling separate and trying to force changes.	Energy released to enjoy life and to creatively change what can be changed. Available energy can be more clearly focused.
Cause-effect reactions to your addictive space—	You perpetuate similar "problems" or addictive patterns in your life.	People's reactions to your preferential love space help create beauty in your life without setting up new problems.

Look at your	Possible suffering and/or rip-offs	As a preference you could experience
Spontaneity, creativity, openness—	Inflexibility; creativity blocked; fearful; pushing and manipulating to attempt to make things happen your way.	Ability to clearly look at "what is" in life and deal with it insightfully. Ability to analyze from a larger perspective.
Alternatives and choices—	Limited; can only see with "tunnel vision"; can only respond automatically and have few options.	Ability to see many beautiful choices in life and be open to a wide variety of possibilities.
Making changes—	Limited because of lack of insight and distorted perception; less energy to effect change.	High energy, clear insight and love create optimal ability to flow energy into changing what is changeable.
When you get what you want—	It is never enough; demands escalate; inability to enjoy because of protecting and defending for fear of losing what you have.	Enjoyment of "what is" in your life; nonattachment to keeping it; loving your life.
Humor—	It seems to be a serious, real and important problem.	You can see humor in the situation; that it's not a serious problem; another situation to watch and enjoy.

ADDICTIVE DEMAND

Write or state your addictive demand using the form:

I create the experience of___(emotions)___because I choose to demand_____.

Our addictive demand is simply our ego and rational mind telling us that "what is" should be different. In most cases that's true, you're absolutely right. But, that doesn't change "what is" in your life.

"WHAT IS"

(This is what you don't want to emotionally accept. Use the same words as in your addictive demand.)

"What is" is what you are emotionally resisting. Being sure to use the same words used in formulating your addictive demand, restate your addictive demand by finishing the sentence: "I am emotionally resisting_____."

EXAMPLES

1. I create the experience of anger and disgust because I choose to demand that I not be 30 pounds overweight.

"What is"

I am emotionally resisting being 30 pounds overweight.

2. I create the experience of sadness, loneliness and hurt because I choose to demand that Bruce not pay more attention to Linda than me.

"What is"

I am emotionally resisting Bruce paying more attention to Linda than me.

In your life, "what is" could be totally accurate, real or factual or it may not even exist in a physical plane reality. It can be imaginary, in the future or totally illusory. Addictive programming creates "what is."

Cover up your addictive demand. Just look at "what is."

See that without this addictive demand, others are able to enjoy or accept the above "what is." Your suffering is caused by your addictive demand, not by "what is."

"What is," no matter what it is, does not cause our suffering. Our addictive demand is the cause of our suffering.

MAKE YOUR CHOICE

Uplevel the addiction to a preference. You can reprogram your addictive demand or uplevel the addiction to a preference.

Preference: A desire that does not make you upset or unhappy if it is not satisfied.

The distinction between an addiction and a preference is in the internal emotional experience, not in the actions, desires, opinions, models or thoughts. When you act preferentially, you emotionally accept what is happening in your life. You might still put a lot of energy into changing it, but you do not feel attached to the results of your actions. You emotionally realize your happiness is not dependent on getting your desire met.

When you reprogram or uplevel your addiction, the following is true:

YOU
— Stop suffering
— Can maintain your opinion
— Can continue trying to change "what is"
— Can still dislike "what is"
— Can more skillfully achieve your positive intention

There is nothing to create suffering, once you eliminate your addictive demand.

You can still put energy into trying to change your situation. You will even be able to change it much more effectively because you are in a preferential space. You'll also have more energy to put into making the changes in this situation.

38

You can still have the opinions you had before. Your models and opinions don't necessarily change when you uplevel your addiction. They just become preferential instead of addictive.

You must emotionally accept "what is," but that doesn't mean you have to like it. You can still want it to be different.

Following is an example of the above points using the addictive demand:

"I choose to create the experience of anger and disgust because I choose to demand that I not be 30 pounds overweight."

As a preference:

I accept that I am 30 pounds overweight.

I do not like being 30 pounds overweight.

I can put energy into dieting or exercise to change my weight.

I can keep my opinion and model that I would rather be trim.

MAKE YOUR CHOICE

Hang on to the addiction:

—You continute to suffer now and in the future.

—"What is" does not change.

If you are experiencing that you still want to hold on to this demand, ask yourself:

"What do I get from hanging on to this demand?"

These are your payoffs. They can be emotional, psychological and/or physical. They can be the rewards that you actually get or they can be the rewards you hope or imagine you'll get. The payoffs can seem ridiculous, untrue and even nonsensical. They also can seem very reasonable, logical and true. Tune-in to the payoffs from holding on to the demand, not the ones that might come from fulfilling the demand.

"I create the experience of anger, disappointment and hurt because I choose to demand that I get a raise."

The payoffs you might get from hanging on to that demand could be:

—You get attention and comfort from people who agree you should get a raise.
—You can be "right."
—You get to blame your boss.
—You can avoid taking responsibility for your situation, feelings, etc.

The payoff would not be that with a raise you can buy a new car or take a trip. That type of payoff comes from getting the raise (getting what you want—your demand satisfied).

Following are some frequent payoffs. They will be useful in helping you pinpoint your own payoffs.

—I get to be right, and make the other person wrong. I get to feel superior. I'll prove it's unfair or untrue.

—I get attention, sympathy, agreement, approval and/or comfort.

—I avoid taking responsibility for what I do, say or feel. I can avoid looking at "what is" in my life. I don't have to really experience what I am feeling.

—People will know that I'm a good (e.g., teacher, responsible person, caring person, bricklayer, etc.).

—People won't think I'm (e.g., egotistical, a coward, etc.).

—I'll have an excuse for poor performance.

—It feels safe to keep the distance from other people (or a specific person). I get to avoid confronting the addictions that would come up if I were close to others.

—It feels safe and familiar to hold on to old programming and scary to let it go.

—I get to enjoy the fantasy. (e.g., "Even if I don't get what I want, I still get to fantasize about it—food, sex.")

—I get to share and feel close to other people who have the same addictions.

—I feel a sense of intensity. (e.g., "I feel really alive when I am angry.")

—I get to be alone. ("If I mope and feel hurt, people will allow me to be alone and not push to be with them.")

—I get control over myself. ("If I demand not to eat, I won't.") I won't do it again. I'll be careful about what I do.

—He/she/they will change. ("If I get angry enough, they'll agree with me or do what I want.") They won't keep doing what they are doing.

—They'll make up to me because they'll see how upset I am and they'll feel bad or guilty.

—I get to be a martyr.

One very illusory payoff that comes up often is "I'll get my way." You've been telling yourself that all your life. Most of the time you can't change things by holding on to your addictive demands. There might be a few times you do. But, at what price? There will still be separation and suffering caused by forcing your way. So you're no happier. You've got what you want and because you got it by force, it sets up the next "problem" or lesson in your life. You still have the addiction. You will have to protect and defend the change you forced. And, you won't be happy. The change won't be "enough." You'll want more and better and longer, and, and, . . . and it doesn't stop.

Begin to notice that all payoffs for holding on to demands are illusory and/or temporary. It often does feel good to feel angry and to feel right, but you can begin to experience the hollowness and separateness that accompanies any "payoff."

These questions can help you get perspective on your "payoffs": (1) Can you see that any "gain" or "loss" in relation to that demand is a temporary experience that does not bring continued inner peace and love in your life? (2) Can you see that you are actually getting less love, peace and energy—and often less of what you are demanding—when you continue to hold on to your addictive demand?

As you look at your "positive intention", does this "payoff" actually help to achieve or maintain the real ultimate feeling you desire?

Look within yourself and see which is more important to you at this moment: to feel loving and close to people, and peaceful in yourself, or to continue to demand what you want.

If you still want to hold on to the demand, you can continue to use this Method by identifying the suffering that keeps coming up with this demand. In the next hours, days, weeks, just keep noticing the suffering and reminding yourself that it's your addiction that is causing it.

Remember!

Hang on to the addiction and
> **—you continue to suffer NOW and in the future**
> **—"what is" does NOT change**

That means because you have not upleveled your demand it will be triggered again and again. Each time you will create suffering and separation in your life.

"What is" remains the same. The only way "what is" changes is when and if you reprogram or uplevel your addiction.

P.S. We all have addictions that we don't want to let go of. When you find yourself holding on to your addiction, love yourself. This is not a race to the finish line.

Be gentle with yourself

EXPLORE YOUR SUFFERING
[Really get into the rip-offs]

Realize that in this here-and-now moment "what is" cannot be changed by you in any way. There is absolutely nothing you can do about it right here and now.

ADDICTIVE DEMAND

Write or state your addictive demand using the form:

"I create the experience of _____

because I choose to demand _____."

"WHAT IS"

This is what you don't want to emotionally accept. Using the same words as in your addictive demand, restate your demand by finishing this sentence: "I am emotionally resisting _____

Cover up your demand. Just look at "what is". See that without this addictive demand, others are able to enjoy or accept the above "what is". Your suffering is caused by your addictive demand, not by "what is".

MAKE YOUR CHOICE

UPLEVEL THE ADDICTION TO A PREFERENCE

— Suffering stops
— You can more skillfully achieve your positive intention
— You can maintain your positive intention
— You can still dislike "what is"
— You can continue to try to change "what is"

HANG ON TO THE ADDICTION

— Suffering continues
— "What is" often remains the same
— It interferes with achieving your positive intention

7

The Catalyst
(All Ways Us Living Love—Method No. 4)

"Use the Catalyst, All Ways Us Living Love, as a tool for cognitive centering."
[*Handbook to Higher Consciousness, page 89*]

By repeating the words of the Catalyst—"All Ways Us Living Love"—your rational mind focuses on those words instead of the addictive programming and mind "chatter" that usually occupies your consciousness. Repeating the Catalyst calms your rational mind when you are caught up in separating emotions.

You can use it until you are calm and centered, or you can use it until you feel calm enough to choose another Method. You can say the Catalyst constantly (you might use a counter to count each time you say it as a reminder and incentive). It becomes a background upon which the events of your day play. This gives perspective to your activities. It can help you feel the "US" place behind all your dramas. The Catalyst also is very effective at calming your mind when you want to go to sleep.

You can use the Catalyst in various ways:

—Say it slowly and silently.

—Emphasize each word successively: **ALL** Ways Us Living Love, All **WAYS** Us Living Love, All Ways **US** Living Love, All Ways Us **LIVING** Love, All Ways Us Living **LOVE**. Put your attention on the word you emphasize. It will help you to keep your rational mind from churning.

—Sing the Catalyst. Singing it aloud or silently keeps your rational mind occupied. Use a tune you know, or make one up.

—Use variations on the Catalyst. They are especially effective when singing it. Here are some suggestions:

Behind all that, here we are.

You give it all up, and you get
it all back.

Life is just a game we play,
and there is no special way.

I love me just the way I am.

I always have everything I need.

I am lovable the way I am.

All-Ways Us Living Love ∿ All Ways Us

Living Love ∿ All Ways Us Living Love

All Ways Us Just Living Love

A word of caution about using the Catalyst to repress separating emotions and addictive programming: It is important to acknowledge separating emotions and the addictive demands that are causing them. After you acknowledge your separating emotions and addictive demands, then use the Catalyst and/or other Living Love Methods to handle or uplevel these addictions.

Practice daily using the Living Love Methods

44

8

Consciousness Focusing
(Method No. 5)

Consciousness Focusing is a dynamic method for breaking away from the old addictive programming that has been creating suffering in your life, and for creatively establishing new loving programs to live with: preferential programs that will create love, oneness and happiness in your life.

First, the most important thing to realize is that you are constantly programming yourself. Everything you tell yourself all day long is programming. For most of your life, you were not in control of just how you were programming yourself. All of your programming was done automatically and unconsciously. Much of this programming was put into your biocomputer when you were emotionally upset.

Everything we tell ourselves when we are emotionally upset has an intense, powerful effect on our biocomputer. By using the Living Love Methods you are now taking charge of what you put in your head. You know that what goes into your head is the programming that determines how you will operate your life.

Your programming creates your emotional experiences. You can use all the Methods, especially Consciousness Focusing, to put into your head loving, preferential programming in place of the addictive programming you have been using.

Consciousness Focusing works most effectively when you have specifically pinpointed your addictive demand. At that point, you know exactly what programming you're telling yourself.

"I create the experience of anger because I choose to demand that Ginger not have lost my earrings."

Consciousness Focusing is your opportunity to change what you're telling yourself by putting a new program into your biocomputer.

"It's OK if Ginger lost my earrings."

"I accept Ginger when she loses my earrings."

The new phrases you put into your biocomputer are called your reprogramming phrases. You are most receptive to them when you have linked your suffering with your addiction.

Be specific!

The first thing you do to use Consciousness Focusing is to determine your reprogramming phrase. The main criterion for a reprogramming phrase is that it feels good to you. The phrase that feels optimal will resonate inside you. You will feel a change in your body, a feeling like, "Yes, that's it. That's the phrase I want to use."

Don't try to convince yourself of something that you can't buy at all rationally. Be sure you can at least accept your phrase on a rational level. Some emotional resistance is to be expected.

When you choose your phrase, use the same wording as in your demand. Make your phrase specific and tie it directly to your addictive demand. Begin with a specific phrase and then, if it flows, you can add a more general phrase to your specific one.

EXAMPLE:

Demand: "I choose to create the experience of anger because I choose to addictively demand that Bill not tell me to empty the garbage."

Specific phrase: "I accept Bill when he tells me to empty the garbage."

General phrase: "I accept Bill when he tells me what to do."

Make your phrase concise, pithy, pointed and rhythmic. Make sure it energizes you, that it is not complicated, intellectual or padded with unnecessary words that don't really add to specificity.

Avoid "I ought to," "I should," "I should not," "I will," "I will not" in your phrases. These statements usually indicate you are rejecting yourself and trying to get rid of the emotion rather than reprogramming the addiction.

Reprogramming works when you deal with upleveling your addictions, not when you're trying to get rid of the emotions. "I want" and "I'll try" are weak and are not strong enough messages to your biocomputer.

Also, avoid judgmental words in your phrases. Perhaps the best guideline is: use a reprogramming phrase that gives your biocomputer a concept you want to live with.

"I create the experience of frustration because I choose to demand I not be 30 pounds overweight."

Don't use "It's OK to be fat." That's not a program you would want to live with.

"I accept myself when I'm 30 pounds heavier than I like."

"I love myself just as I am."

If you can't rationally accept a phrase with "I accept" or "I love" because it seems a little too strong, add "am learning to."

"I am learning to love myself just as I am."

Reprogramming phrases usually will flow straight from the wording of your addictive demand.

If you have difficulty selecting a reprogramming phrase, go back to your addictive demand. Check first to make sure your demand is specific. Make sure the demand is the one that is triggering your separating emotions. Sometimes we have to "search" for a phrase because we are not working on the demand that is really bothering us.

If the demand feels right to you, and a reprogramming phrase doesn't come easily, try some of the "suggested phrases." Adjust them to fit your particular addictive demand.

Some suggested phrases:

Addictive Demand: "I create the experience of anger because I choose to demand that Kevin not spill his milk."

"I am learning to love Kevin when he spills his milk."

"I love and accept Kevin when he spills his milk."

"It's OK for Kevin to spill his milk."

"I am learning to accept Kevin when he spills his milk."

"I love (accept) Kevin when he spills his milk."

If you still can't find a phrase that feels right to you, ask yourself: "Do I really believe that this addiction is the cause of my suffering?" "Do I want to reprogram this addiction?"

Be honest with yourself. If you don't really see that your suffering is caused by your addictive demand, go through the Link the Suffering with the Addiction form again.

If you don't want to reprogram your demand, that's fine. Don't keep fooling yourself. There's no need to use the Methods if you don't want to get free of your addictions.

Remember: When forming your reprogramming phrases:

1. Be specific.

2. Form phrases that are pithy, rhythmic and catchy.

3. Be sure the phrase feels good to you.

4. Be sure the phrase makes sense to your rational mind.

5. Avoid using such words as "should," "shouldn't," "ought" or "I will."

6. Be careful not to include judgmental hooks ["even if . . ."].

7. Make sure your phrase is directly related to your addictive demand. If your reprogramming phrase feels "right on" and does not relate to your addictive demand, go back and reformulate your addictive demand.

Once you've chosen a phrase you can accept, the next step is to repeat it over and over to firmly establish it in your biocomputer.

Consciousness Focusing as a Method

There are four ways Consciousness Focusing can be used as a Living Love Method. Your choice depends upon the emotional intensity associated with your addictive demand.

1. Repeat your reprogramming phrases quietly and meditatively. This is an excellent way to use Consciousness Focusing. It can be extremely effective just before going to sleep or immediately upon waking in the morning. Breathe deeply and relax. Then quietly and meditatively repeat your phrase over and over. You also can take time during the day to quiet your mind and repeat your phrase for several minutes.

2. Repeat the reprogramming phrase as you go about your daily activities. Consciousness Focusing can be done entirely in your head anytime, any place. Pick a reprogramming phrase, then repeat it over and over in your head. Use the phrase constantly during the day. Write your phrase(s) down, put them around your home, in your car, even at work, to remind you to repeat the phrase. Like the Catalyst, the reprogramming phrase can become the background against which the events of your day play. Increase the intensity by silently yelling in your head, and/or by tensing some of your muscles or your whole body.

3. Repeat the reprogramming phrase when you are doing intense physical exercise. This practice uses the adrenalin that is in your system when you do an intense physical activity, such as jogging, jumping, running, swimming, biking, just about anything active and/or aerobic. The adrenalin in your body helps the new program to make a solid connection in your biocomputer. As you are involved in the activity, yell your reprogramming phrase either silently in your head or aloud. This method of Consciousness Focusing can be extremely powerful.

4. Use the classic way of Consciousness Focusing: yell your reprogramming phrase while you are experiencing intense, heavy emotions. You may be crying, or about to, your body is shaking, or lots of adrenalin is pumping in your system. This way of Consciousness Focusing is very effective when you feel the need to really express your opinion.

With your reprogramming phrase in mind, look back over all the suffering your demand has caused you in your life. Feel how deeply you want to reprogram the addiction that is causing all your suffering. Really build the intensity. Experience how tired you are of all this suffering.

Tense your body, perhaps clench your fists. Get on your knees, either on the floor with a pillow in front of you or on the bed. Lower your head; really intensify your feelings as you continue to tense your body. Start by silently screaming your phrase in your head. Then, if you want, start screaming aloud. Beat the pillow or your bed. Really get into expressing yourself. Keep it going as long as you can.

You may want to make your own Consciousness Focusing tool. Yell into a plastic waste paper basket with a sponge in the bottom. This decreases the sound for your neighbors and increases the sound of your reprogramming phrase as it goes into your biocomputer.

Whenever you experience intense emotional feelings, take the opportunity to use Consciousness Focusing. Any time you are emotionally upset you have a valuable opportunity to put new programming into your biocomputer. It bypasses your ego and rational mind more easily. It is possible to reprogram years of negative programming in a relatively short time with Consciousness Focusing.

But remember, most of your addictive programming has been with you a long time. You have lived with and operated from it for many years. Be patient with yourself. Don't expect to uplevel years of addictive programming to preferential programming overnight.

Here's a list of some effective words to use to begin your reprogramming phrase:
- — I am learning to accept...
- — I am learning to love...
- — I can accept...
- — I can love...
- — I accept...
- — I love...
- — I love and accept...
- — I can be happy when...
- — I can feel peaceful when...
- — It's OK...
- — I'm OK...
- — I can feel (plug in your positive intention) when...

You may also find it effective to substitute "you" for "I" in the above reprogramming phrase beginnings and talk to yourself, e.g., "You can accept...," "You can learn to love..." You can also use your name, e.g., "Kris, you can love yourself..."

You might benefit from using names and pet names you had as a child, since much of your programming was addressed and absorbed by "that person". In addition, if another language was used by you or around you during childhood, try Consciousness Focusing in that language.

Be gentle with yourself

9

Instant Consciousness Doubler

The Instant Consciousness Doubler can take you behind the programming and into that "us" place, where we all are one. It helps you to start realizing that your programming and behavior are just "drama." It's not who you really are. As you use the Instant Consciousness Doubler, you learn how we are all trapped by our automatic, addictive programming. The Instant Consciousness Doubler will deepen your compassion, not only for the other people in your life, but also for yourself. At The Ken Keyes Center we use the Instant Consciousness Doubler in several ways. First way:

—Pick a person from whom you feel separate.

—Pinpoint what he/she does which you use to create separation from him/her.

—Tune-in to the space you create when you are totally loving and accepting of yourself.

—With that space in your mind, recall when you were in a similar situation and reacting in a similar way, saying and/or doing the same or similar things. Experience the love and acceptance you have for yourself.

—Expand that love and compassion to include the other person.

In cases where you just can't imagine that you would ever act or be like the other person, try using the Instant Consciousness Doubler another way:

—Put yourself into the space of the person you feel separate from. Really get into his/her head.

—Look at his/her programming. Imagine having the exact programming she/he has. It's now your programming.

—Realize that most of our programming gives us no choice in the way we act.

—See how with his/her exact programming, you would have acted in the same manner.

—Tune-in to that space where you have love and compassion for yourself, even when you're trapped by your addictive programming.

— Expand that love and compassion to include the other person. Remember, we are all victims of our programming. It's only when we become conscious of how our programming controls our lives and choose to take charge of that programming that we begin to get free of our robot-like behavior.

We know that every person has a positive intention behind each thought, action, and statement. This provides another way to implement the Instant Consciousness Doubler:

— Imagine that other person's possible positive intention.
— See their actions and words as an unskillful attempt to achieve their positive intention.
— Remember how often you, too, fall into unskillful attempts at achieving your positive intentions.
— Pinpoint what you have said or done that causes you to feel separate from yourself.
— See that you are simply acting out your addictive programming.
— Tune-in to the love and acceptance you have felt for others when they have done a similar thing, when they acted out their addictive programming. You did not put them out of your heart or criticize them.
— Identify your positive intention in that situation. Realize how understandable that intention is and feel compassion for yourself and the unskillful attempt you made at achieving that intention.
— Expand your love and compassion to include yourself. See that you can be as loving and patient with yourself as you are with others. You can give yourself the same space you give others.

Many people use this Method without being aware that they are doing it. We can remind ourselves to use the Instant Consciousness Doubler by singing it.

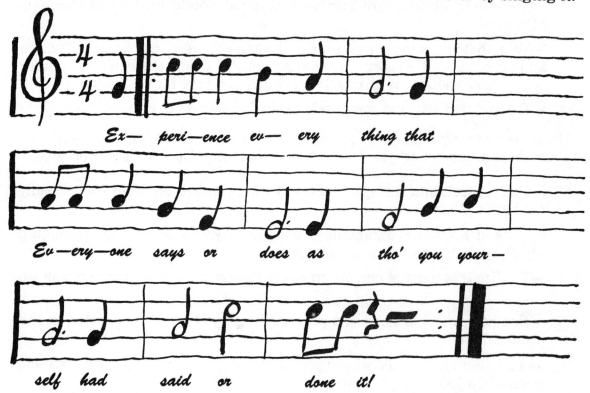

Ex— peri—ence ev— ery thing that

Ev—ery—one says or does as tho' you your—

self had said or done it!

Many people will use the Instant Consciousness Doubler automatically on separation they create with others, but not on separation they feel with themselves. Practice all the different ways of using the ICD. It can be an important tool for helping you uplevel your judgmentalness, both of yourself and of other people.

Enjoy your journey

Be gentle with yourself

10

Addictive Snarl

An addictive snarl occurs when our biocomputers become bogged down in multiple or conflicting addictions. Our emotional state at these times is referred to as depression, feeling inadequate, generalized boredom or anxiety. We're aware of feeling separate from ourselves and others. We know we're definitely not enjoying life. Yet, we are not aware of any specific addiction that may be causing this emotional condition. When we think back over the people and situations we've been interacting with, we may not be able to zero in on any incidents significant enough to have triggered this mental state.

When we don't handle our addictions one by one, we build them up to a point of emotional overload. When this happens we "blow a fuse" and shut down emotionally. We remain "grayed out" until we reduce the overload.

Here are some suggestions for untangling an addictive snarl and getting back to the business of enjoying your life:

If your addictive snarl has lots of emotion involved,

[1] Use the Catalyst, All Ways Us Living Love, to calm the churning of your rational mind. You may want to continue that for a period of time, or you may want to calm your mind to the point where you choose another Method.

[2] Simply say the Pathways slowly and meditatively, one by one, aloud if you can. If you still have a lot of emotion when you finish saying them, say them again.

You also can:

[1] Take several deep breaths and let yourself relax. Let your mind travel back to focus on the time when the confusion or depression began. When you don't pay attention to your feelings, addictions begin to pile up, creating snarls. What was happening when you began to feel uptight or uncomfortable? Sometimes addictive snarls are created to avoid looking at what is really bothering you. After you focus on the time when the uptightness began, then pinpoint one specific addictive demand. Identify your positive intention and use one or more of the Methods.

[2] To find out what's bothering you, make a list of all of your demands—heavy ones, small "niggles," subtle addictions. List all the things that you would like changed in your life. When you have finished your list, choose the one specific addictive demand that has the most emotional energy—the one which upsets you the most. **Work on that demand using one or more of the Methods.**

[3] Do an EIP using the incident where you are now. EIP is an excellent process for sorting through your addictive programming to select your addictive demand. You may wish to go more thoroughly into Step C, "What am I telling myself?"

Practice! Practice! Practice!

Use the Methods

Be gentle with yourself

11

Exploration Insight Process

The Exploration Insight Process helps you to gain clarity and insight when you are feeling separating emotions. It is a way of organizing and sorting through the programming that your rational mind and ego start running when an addictive demand is triggered. It helps you find the central addictive demand that is creating your suffering. And the EIP can help you to gain new perspective and insights to uplevel your addictions into preferences.

You can use the EIP anytime and anywhere, whenever you experience separating emotions. It can be especially helpful with recurring addictive demand patterns that you want more insight about, when you feel tension in your body and want to explore the programming that produces it, or when you have trouble pinpointing your addictive demands. Experiment with the Exploration Insight Process. Learn how and when it works most effectively for you.

There are six steps in the Exploration Insight Process. Memorize these steps so you can use the process easily.

The Exploration Insight Process can take a minute or two, an hour or two, or anywhere in between. You can do it silently, aloud or in writing. You can use it alone or share it with one or more people.

When you are doing an EIP, do each of the steps in turn. Build each step on the previous ones. Any one of the steps by itself can let you have the insight you need to uplevel a demand or let go of it.

> ## Exploration Insight Process (EIP)
>
> A. Incident
>
> B. Physical sensations/emotions
>
> C. What am I telling myself?
>
> D. Demand(s)
>
> E. Positive intention
>
> F. Living Love Method(s)

Stay in the present tense, even if you are recalling an incident from the past. If the incident is from the past, re-experience your feelings and imagine yourself back in the actual situation. Do each step of the Exploration Insight Process as if you were right in the midst of the incident. When you do an EIP at the time you feel upset, you can simply observe what is happening as you do each step.

If you are going through the EIP aloud, it works better to keep your eyes closed so you can stay in tune with your feelings and with what is going on in your mind. Even if you're writing, ask yourself the questions, close your eyes and tune-in to your feelings and thoughts. Practice using the EIP. Practice doing it aloud. Practice it silently. Practice writing it. You will gain speed, skill and a sense of when and how an EIP works most effectively for you.

The following explanation of the Exploration Insight Process includes useful questions to ask yourself (left-hand column) and the purpose of the step (right-hand column). Review it often. This information and the use of the EIP will enable you to become more and more aware of your addictive programming.

Exploration Insight Process

A. Incident

PROCEDURE

(Answer the following questions briefly.)

Who is involved?

Where is it happening?

What is happening?

What is being said?

PURPOSE

The objective description of the situation helps you to see the illusion that is created as your addictive programming interprets that event. It gives you new perspective and insight.

Be specific and pinpoint the exact words, actions or thoughts that triggered your feelings. Always be brief, factual, concise, simple. Don't get into your physical sensations, emotions or thoughts in this first step.

B. Physical sensations/emotions

PROCEDURE

Put yourself back in the incident when you talk about your physical sensations and emotions.

Always speak in the present tense. "Where do I feel tension, discomfort or shaking in my body?" (Check your head, neck, throat, shoulders, chest, back, stomach, intestines, legs. Notice tears, the sound of your voice and speed of your breath.) "Which emotions am I feeling?" (See list of separating emotions on page 28.)

PURPOSE

Tunes you in to body tensions and specific emotions. Helps you become aware of what you are telling yourself. It will help in pinpointing your demand and in using the Methods. You simply acknowledge and experience what you are feeling without defending, judging or explaining yourself.

Don't explain "why," qualify or use general emotions. "Because of," "the reason is" don't belong in this step. Notice if you use general terms like

58

"separate," "alienated," "unhappy" or "uncomfortable." Get in touch with the specific separating emotions that are involved. Don't qualify your emotions. "I guess I feel" or "a little angry" are ways your ego tries to avoid experiencing or acknowledging what you really feel.

C. What am I telling myself?

PROCEDURE

"What am I telling myself that creates the experience of (emotion from Step B)?" "What do I really want in this situation?" "How do I want things to be?"

Additional questions that might be helpful are:

What's bothering me the most?

What are my models of how things should be or shouldn't be?

If things go the way I want, what does it mean about me?

If things don't go the way I want, what does it mean about me?

How would I change in this situation?

What do I think I (he/she) should have done or shouldn't have done?

How do I feel about what is happening?

What is it about me that can't be loved?

Questions that are especially helpful in relation to particular emotions:

Fear:

What's the worst thing that could happen?

Imagine that happened: Now what's the worst thing?

What am I avoiding?

What am I hiding?

What is the threat in this situation?

PURPOSE

To become aware of and express the addictive programming that is triggered by the incident. It helps you experience your central demand. You also become familiar with how your addictive programming works to cause your suffering.

Guilt:

What should I have done? felt?

What would I do if I were completely free in this situation?

How do I feel about that?

Boredom, frustration or disappointment:

What do I want to be happening?

What would have to be happening so I wouldn't feel bored, etc.?

Anger:

What am I protecting, defending?

What would happen if I didn't control?

How do I feel about myself, about other people when I can't control?

If the person keeps doing what she/he is doing, what might happen?

Say what comes into your mind, no matter how silly, absurd, wrong, right, unreasonable, untrue, impossible, illogical, irrational, petty or unfair it seems. Do not censor or limit expressing your addictive programming. Don't try to look good or look conscious. Don't try to analyze or rationalize away what you are feeling by explaining what you know intellectually to be true.

"Well, I know I really don't have to feel this way, and it's kind of silly." Keep the incident in your mind and continue to ask yourself: "What am I telling myself that is creating feelings of (anger, fear, jealousy, etc.)?"

D. Demand(s)

PROCEDURE

Pinpoint your addictive demands using the form: I create the experience of (emotions) because I choose to addictively demand (what you want).

PURPOSE

To look at your various addictive demand(s) which are causing you the most suffering. This helps you to use the Methods in Step F more effectively.

List several addictive demands. Choose the one that is bothering you the most. If you don't feel you can select one, you may want to go back and explore further Step C, "What am I telling myself?"

E. Positive Intention

(How would you feel if you actually got that demand satisfied, if things went the way you wanted?)

My positive intention behind this demand is to feel _____
(or)
My positive intention behind this demand is to see myself as _____

_____

F. Living Love Methods

PROCEDURE

1. The Twelve Pathways
2. Centers of Consciousness
3. Link the Suffering With the Addiction
4. Catalyst—Always Us Living Love
5. Consciousness Focusing
6. Instant Consciousness Doubler

PURPOSE

To use the Methods to gain insight so you can uplevel your addiction to a preference, reprogram your addictive demand or recognize that you are not willing to let go of the addictive demand at this time.

All the Living Love Methods are explained in detail in the Methods section. Experiment with all the Methods, both individually and with various combinations to find what works best for you.

Memorize these steps:

A. Incident
B. Physical sensations/emotions
C. What am I telling myself?
D. Demand(s)
E. Positive Intention
F. Living Love Method(s)

Practice! Practice! Practice!

HAVE PATIENCE! And Remember:

The Methods Work . . . if you do!

12

Written Exploration Insight Process

Writing out the Exploration Insight Process can be extremely helpful and insightful. It is especially useful if you're having trouble keeping your mind focused when working alone. Writing out an EIP can give you added perspective and help you recognize that it's all just your programming. And your programming has nothing to do with who you really are.

When you have time, it is recommended you write three pages or more of Step C, "What Am I Telling Myself?" This extra effort helps you get into all the programming you won't usually look deep enough to see.

Always choose the Method that you feel works most effectively for you. If one doesn't seem to work, try another. Some addictive demands might require you to use all of the Methods before you gain the insight necessary to "handle the addiction"—or eventually uplevel the addictive demand to a preference.

The printed forms that follow are helpful, but they are not necessary to use the Exploration Insight Process. These forms are examples of the written EIP form and how each Living Love Method may be used with the written EIP.

Exploration Insight Process (EIP)

    A. Incident

    B. Physical sensations/emotions

    C. What am I telling myself?

    D. Demand(s)

    E. Positive Intention

    F. Living Love Method(s)

(Following are Written Exploration Insight Process practice sheets. Each contains the six steps of the process and designates one or more of the Living Love Methods to use. Choose your Method or Methods on the last practice sheet.)

Written EIP No. 1—The Pathways as the Method

Words in bold face are to aid you in each step. It is not necessary to answer all of the questions to do steps A, B, C, D, E, and F. It is helpful to read all the questions before you do each step. Be sure to do both pages-notice that any Method can be used in Step F.

A. INCIDENT
(Who is involved? Where is it happening? What is happening? What is being said?)

B. PHYSICAL SENSATIONS/EMOTIONS
(If you want help, use some of these questions: Am I feeling tension in my head, throat, neck, shoulders, chest, back, stomach, intestines, legs, anywhere in my body? Am I crying? How does my voice sound? Which of these emotions am I feeling: fear, worry, anxiety, terror, guilt, horror, panic, disappointment, hurt, confusion, sadness, embarrassment, shame, grief, apprehension, loneliness, jealousy, boredom, frustration, disgust, disdain, fury, indignation, impatience, anger, hatred, resentment?)

C. WHAT AM I TELLING MYSELF?
(If you don't feel you have become aware of what is really triggering your emotions, you can use some of these questions: What is the worst thing that could happen in this situation? What is bothering me the most? What are my models of how things should be or shouldn't be? If things go the way I want, what do I get? If things don't go the way I want, what do I get? What would I change in this situation? What do I feel other people are going to think? What do I want to be happening? What do I think I should have done? What threat does this situation pose to me? How do I feel about what is happening?)

What else am I telling myself?

D. DEMAND(S)
(If you don't feel you have pinpointed the addictive demand that is triggering the emotions you are feeling, you can use these questions to help you: **If a magic genie appeared, what would I ask for in this situation? [The magic genie can grant you any one wish.] What is it I feel I need to be happy in this situation? How do I feel things should be [or I should be] or shouldn't be in this situation?**)

I CREATE THE EXPERIENCE OF_____ (emotions) _____

_____

BECAUSE I CHOOSE TO DEMAND: _____

_____

E. POSITIVE INTENTION
(How would you feel if you actually got that demand satisfied, if things went the way you wanted?)

My positive intention behind this demand is to feel _____
(or)
My positive intention behind this demand is to see myself as _____

_____

F. LIVING LOVE METHOD[S]: Method No. 1: The Twelve Pathways
Say all twelve Pathways. Say one or more Pathways over and over. Say your addictive demand and one Pathway alternately or say your addictive demand alternately with each of the Pathways.

Written EIP No. 2—Centers of Consciousness as the Method

Words in bold face are to aid you in each step. It is not necessary to answer all of the questions to do steps A, B, C, D, E, and F. It is helpful to read all the questions before you do each step. Be sure to do both pages-notice that any Method can be used in Step F.

A. INCIDENT
(Who is involved? Where is it happening? What is happening? What is being said?)

B. PHYSICAL SENSATIONS/EMOTIONS
(If you want help, use some of these questions: **Am I feeling tension in my head, throat, neck, shoulders, chest, back, stomach, intestines, legs, anywhere in my body? Am I crying? How does my voice sound? Which of these emotions am I feeling: fear, worry, anxiety, terror, guilt, horror, panic, disappointment, hurt, confusion, sadness, embarrassment, shame, grief, apprehension, loneliness, jealousy, boredom, frustration, disgust, disdain, fury, indignation, impatience, anger, hatred, resentment?**)

C. WHAT AM I TELLING MYSELF?
(If you don't feel you have become aware of what is really triggering your emotions, you can use some of these questions: **What is the worst thing that could happen in this situation? What is bothering me the most? What are my models of how things should be or shouldn't be? If things go the way I want, what do I get? If things don't go the way I want, what do I get? What would I change in this situation? What do I feel other people are going to think? What do I want to be happening? What do I think I should have done? What threat does this situation pose to me? How do I feel about what is happening?**)

What else am I telling myself?

D. DEMAND(s)
(If you don't feel you have pinpointed the addictive demand that is triggering the emotions you are feeling, you can use these questions to help you: **If a magic genie appeared, what would I ask for in this situation? (The magic genie can grant you any one wish.) What is it I feel I need to be happy in this situation? What would I like to change in this situation? How do I feel things should be [or I should be] or shouldn't be in this situation?)**

I CREATE THE EXPERIENCE OF _____(emotions)_____
_____

BECAUSE I CHOOSE TO DEMAND:_____
_____

E. POSITIVE INTENTION
(How would you feel if you actually got that demand satisfied, if things went the way you wanted?)

My positive intention behind this demand is to feel _____ .
(or)
My positive intention behind this demand is to see myself as _____
_____

F. LIVING LOVE METHOD[S]: Method No. 2: Centers of Consciousness
Notice your center of consciousness when you feel uptight; replay the same scene through centers 1, 2, 3, 4, 5, 6 or just through centers 4, 5, 6.

Written EIP No. 3—Link the Suffering With the Addiction and Consciousness Focusing as the Methods

Words in bold face are to aid you in each step. It is not necessary to answer all of the questions to do steps A, B, C, D, E, and F. It is helpful to read all the questions before you do each step. Be sure to do both pages-notice that any Method can be used in Step F.

A. INCIDENT
(**Who is involved? Where is it happening? What is happening? What is being said?**)

B. PHYSICAL SENSATIONS/EMOTIONS
(If you want help, use some of these questions: **Am I feeling tension in my head, throat, neck, shoulders, chest, back, stomach, intestines, legs, anywhere in my body? Am I crying? How does my voice sound? Which of these emotions am I feeling: fear, worry, anxiety, terror, guilt, nervousness, horror, panic, disappointment, hurt, confusion, sadness, embarrassment, shame, grief, apprehension, loneliness, jealousy, boredom, frustration, disdain, fury, indignation, impatience, anger, hatred, resentment?**)

C. WHAT AM I TELLING MYSELF?
(If you don't feel you have become aware of what is really triggering your emotions, you can use some of these questions: **What is the worst thing that could happen in this situation? What is bothering me the most? What are my models of how things should be or shouldn't be? If things go the way I want, what do I get? If things don't go the way I want, what do I get? What would I change in this situation? What do I feel other people are going to think? What do I want to be happening? What do I think I should have done? What threat does this situation pose to me? How do I feel about what is happening?**)

What else am I telling myself?

D. DEMAND(S)
(If you don't feel you have pinpointed the addictive demand that is triggering the emotions you are feeling, you can use these questions to help you: **If a magic genie appeared, what would I ask for in this situation? (The magic genie can grant you any one wish.) What is it I feel I need to be happy in this situation? What would I like to change in this situation? How do I feel things should be [or I should be] or shouldn't be in this situation?**)

I CREATE THE EXPERIENCE OF_____(emotions)_____
_____
BECAUSE I CHOOSE TO DEMAND:_____
_____

E. POSITIVE INTENTION
(How would you feel if you actually got that demand satisfied, if things went the way you wanted?)

My positive intention behind this demand is to feel _____
(or)
My positive intention behind this demand is to see myself as _____
_____

F. LIVING LOVE METHOD[S]: Method No. 3: Link the Suffering With the Addiction

EXPLORE YOUR SUFFERING
(Really get into the rip-offs)
"WHAT IS"
Restate your addictive demand (use the same words as in your addictive demand): "I am emotionally resisting_____
_____."

Realize that in this here-and-now moment "what is" cannot be changed by you in any way. There is absolutely nothing you can do about it right here and now. See that without this addictive demand others are able to enjoy or accept the above "what is." Your suffering is caused by your addictive demand, not by "what is."

MAKE YOUR CHOICE

| UPLEVEL THE ADDICTION TO A PREFERENCE | HANG ON TO THE ADDICTION (If this is your choice, what are the payoffs you get from hanging on to the demand?) |

F. LIVING LOVE METHOD[S]: Method No. 5: Consciousness Focusing
Choose a reprogramming phrase. Make sure it relates directly to your demand and that it feels good to you.

69

Words in bold face are to aid you in each step. It is not necessary to answer all of the questions to do steps A, B, C, D, E, and F. It is helpful to read all the questions before you do each step. Be sure to do both pages-notice that any Method can be used in Step F.

A. INCIDENT

(Who is involved? Where is it happening? What is happening? What is being said?)

B. PHYSICAL SENSATIONS/EMOTIONS

(If you want help, use some of these questions: **Am I feeling tension in my head, throat, neck, shoulders, chest, back, stomach, intestines, legs, anywhere in my body? Am I crying? How does my voice sound? Which of these emotions am I feeling: fear, worry, anxiety, terror, guilt, horror, panic, disappointment, hurt, confusion, sadness, embarrassment, shame, grief, apprehension, loneliness, jealousy, boredom, frustration, disgust, disdain, fury, indignation, impatience, anger, hatred, resentment?)**

C. WHAT AM I TELLING MYSELF?

(If you don't feel you have become aware of what is really triggering your emotions, you can use some of these questions: **What is the worst thing that could happen in this situation? What is bothering me the most? What are my models of how things should be or shouldn't be? If things go the way I want, what do I get? If things don't go the way I want, what do I get? What would I change in this situation? What do I feel other people are going to think? What do I want to be happening? What do I think I should have done? What threat does this situation pose to me? How do I feel about what is happening?)**

What else am I telling myself?

D. DEMAND(S)

(If you don't feel you have pinpointed the addictive demand that is triggering the emotions you are feeling, you can use these questions to help you: **If a magic genie appeared, what would I ask for in this situation?** (The magic genie can grant you any **one** wish.) **What is it I feel I need to be happy in this situation? What would I like to change in this situation? How do I feel things should be (or I should be) or shouldn't be in this situation?**)

I CREATE THE EXPERIENCE OF _____
                                        (emotions)
_____

BECAUSE I CHOOSE TO DEMAND: _____
_____

E. POSITIVE INTENTION

(How would you feel if you actually got that demand satisfied, if things went the way you wanted?)

My positive intention behind this demand is to feel _____
(or)
My positive intention behind this demand is to see myself as _____
_____

F. LIVING LOVE METHOD(S): Method No. 4: The Catalyst (All Ways Us Living Love)

Say the Catalyst slowly and silently. Emphasize each word successively: ALL Ways Us Living Love; All WAYS Us Living Love; All Ways US Living Love; All Ways Us LIVING Love; All Ways Us Living LOVE. Sing it (aloud **or** silently), using variations on the words (e.g., "I love me just the way I am").

71

Written EIP No. 5 — Instant Consciousness Doubler as the Method

Words in bold face are to aid you in each step. It is not necessary to answer all of the questions to do steps A, B, C, D, E, and F. It is helpful to read all the questions before you do each step. Be sure to do both pages-notice that any Method can be used in Step F.

A. INCIDENT

(**Who is involved? Where is it happening? What is happening? What is being said?**)

B. PHYSICAL SENSATIONS/EMOTIONS

(If you want help, use some of these questions: **Am I feeling tension in my head, throat, neck, shoulders, chest, back, stomach, intestines, legs, anywhere in any body? Am I crying? How does my voice sound? Which of these emotions am I feeling: fear, worry, anxiety, terror, guilt, nervousness, horror, panic, disappointment, hurt, confusion, sadness, embarrassment, shame, grief, apprehension, loneliness, jealousy, boredom, frustration, disgust, disdain, fury, indignation, impatience, anger, hatred, resentment?**)

C. WHAT AM I TELLING MYSELF?

(If you don't feel you have become aware of what is really triggering your emotions, you can use some of these questions: **What is the worst thing that could happen in this situation? What is bothering me the most? What are my models of how things should be or shouldn't be? If things go the way I want, what do I get? If things don't go the way I want, what do I get? What would I change in this situation? What do I feel other people are going to think? What do I want to be happening? What do I think I should have done? What threat does this situation pose to me? How do I feel about what is happening?**)

D. DEMAND(S)

(If you don't feel you have pinpointed the addictive demand that is triggering the emotions you are feeling, you can use these questions to help you: **If a magic genie appeared, what would I ask for in this situation? (The magic genie can grant you any one wish.) What is it I feel I need to be happy in this situation? What would I like to change in this situation? How do I feel things should be [or I should be] or shouldn't be in this situation?**)

I CREATE THE EXPERIENCE OF_____
                                                          (emotions)
_____
BECAUSE I CHOOSE TO DEMAND:_____

_____

E. POSITIVE INTENTION

(How would you feel if you actually got that demand satisfied, if things went the way you wanted?)

My positive intention behind this demand is to feel _____
(or)
My positive intention behind this demand is to see myself as _____

_____

F. LIVING LOVE METHODS: Instant Consciousness Doubler

Tune-in to the space you create when you're totally loving and accepting of yourself. See that you have the potential to do or have done the same thing as the person you feel separate from. Expand your own love and compassion to include them.

Written EIP No. 6 — Choose your Method(s)

A. INCIDENT

B. PHYSICAL SENSATIONS/EMOTIONS

C. WHAT AM I TELLING MYSELF?

D. DEMAND[S]

E. POSITIVE INTENTION

F. LIVING LOVE METHOD[S]

13

Shared Exploration Insight Process

At times it is helpful to share the Exploration Insight Process with another person. This section is an outline to guide two people through an Exploration Insight Process. The person doing the EIP is the speaker, and the person guiding is the listener.

The listener guides the speaker by reading each step, giving the speaker time to respond in each situation. The information in parentheses ( ) provides directions for the listener. Once you become thoroughly familiar with the process, you can ask other "helpful questions," or vary the amount of time spent on any step.

As a listener, the most supportive thing you can do is give the speaker your loving attention and energy while he/she does this process. Advice, insights (aside from the feedback indicated) and stories of your experiences distract the speaker from the inner work he/she is doing.

Start by sitting and facing one another. Bring your energy together by putting your arms around each other and breathing in unison.

A. Incident

Listener says, "Close your eyes and take a deep breath. Focus on an incident in which you felt separating emotions. See the actual situation in your mind's eye. Give a factual description of that scene by answering these questions briefly:

"Who is involved?
"Where is it happening?
"What is happening? What is being said?"

B. Physical sensations/emotions

Listener says, "Take a deep breath. Imagine that you are right in that scene. Speak in the present tense. How does your body feel?" (Listener, remind the speaker of body areas where he/she might be holding tension, including breathing and any other physical manifestations you notice.) "Are you feeling tension in your head, throat, neck, shoulders, chest, back, stomach, intestines, legs, anywhere in your body? Do you want to cry? How does your voice sound?"

"Which of these emotions are you feeling: fear, worry, anxiety, guilt, nervousness, horror, terror, panic, disappointment, hurt, confusion, sadness, embarrassment, shame, grief, apprehension, loneliness, jealousy, boredom, frustration, disgust, disdain, fury, indignation, impatience, anger, hatred, resentment?''

C. What are you telling yourself?

Listener says, "What are you telling yourself that makes you feel that emotion?'' (fear, anger, etc. Use the specific emotion(s) the speaker stated. If appropriate, listener might also ask) "What is the worst thing that could happen in this situation? What is bothering you the most? What are your models of how things should be or shouldn't be? If things go the way you want, what do you get? If things don't go the way you want, what do you get? What would you change in this situation? What do you feel other people are going to think? What do you want to be happening? What do you think you should have done? What does this mean about you? How do you feel about what is happening?'' (Encourage the speaker to get into all the things he/she is telling him/herself.)

D. Addictive demand[s]

Listener says, "What are you addictively demanding? What do you really want in this situation? If a magic genie appeared, what would you ask for in this situation? (The magic genie can grant you any **one** wish.) What is it you feel you need to be happy in this situation? What would you like to change in this situation? How do you feel things should be (or you should be) or shouldn't be in this situation?''
(Listener, write down all the speaker's addictive demands.) Formulate your major addictive demand: "**I create the experience of** (separating emotions) **because I choose to demand_____.''**

(Listener now gives feedback, using the form) "**I perceive that you are creating the experience of** (separating emotions) **because you are demanding** (what listener feels he/she is demanding).''

Listener says, "Choose a specific addictive demand that you want to work on and restate it.'' (Listener, write the demand.)

E. Positive Intention

Listener says, "Behind this demand there is a beneficial positive intention. If you were to get this demand satisfied, how would you feel? How might you see yourself if you got what you wanted?''

(Listener write down the positive intention using the form): "My positive intention behind this demand is to feel _____; (or) to see myself as _____ .''

F. Living Love Method(s)

Listener says, "Which Method(s) would you like to use with this demand to help you claim your positive intention?''

THE TWELVE PATHWAYS

Listener says, if necessary,

"Recite the Pathway(s) that would be most helpful to you in this situation," and/or

"Say all twelve Pathways," and/or

"Say your positive intention and one Pathway alternately several times."

THE CENTERS OF CONSCIOUSNESS

Listener says, if necessary,

"Which center(s) of consciousness are you using to create your experience of this scene? and/or

"Now imagine and share what it would be like to experience that situation from the first four (or more) centers of consciousness."

LINK THE SUFFERING WITH THE ADDICTION

Listener says, "Explore your suffering. Look at all the ways your enjoyment is being ripped off."

Listener says, "Pinpoint your specific addictive demand."

Listener says, "Restate your addictive demand as your emotional resistance to 'what is' in your life. Use the form, 'I am emotionally resisting_____.' "

Listener says, "Realize that in this here-and-now moment 'what is' cannot be changed by you in any way. There is absolutely nothing you can do about it right here and now. By continuing to emotionally resist 'what is' you will only perpetuate your suffering."

Listener says, "Now describe the same incident in which you triggered your addictive demand, only this time do not emotionally resist 'what is.' Remember, nothing changes in the incident, except your suffering is gone."

Listener says, "When you experience yourself still unwilling to emotionally accept 'what is' it is because 'payoffs' are preventing you from seeing that all of your suffering is being caused by your addiction. Identify the payoffs to discover what you are telling yourself you are getting by continuing to emotionally resist 'what is.' "

Listener says, "All payoffs perpetuate separateness. Give yourself permission to hold on to your addiction, but practice seeing through the illusion cast by the payoffs. Describe how the payoffs actually keep you stuck in (1) isolation, (2) crystallized opinions of yourself and others and (3) suffering."

CONSCIOUSNESS FOCUSING

Listener says, "Restate your demand and choose reprogramming phrase(s)." (Listener, suggest phrases.) "Which phrase feels best to you?" (Listener, write down this phrase.)

—After the speaker gets into a reprogramming position, **Listener says,** "Tense your muscles and breathe deeply. Feel all of the suffering that this addiction has caused you, over and over in your life. Use your emotional energy and say your phrase over and over again with intensity and determination. (Listener, get into reprogramming position and reprogram silently or aloud with your partner.)

THE CATALYST

Listener says, "Say the Catalyst slowly and silently. Emphasize each word successively: ALL Ways Us Living Love; All WAYS Us Living Love; All Ways US Living Love; All Ways Us LIVING Love; All Ways Us Living LOVE."

INSTANT CONSCIOUSNESS DOUBLER

Listener says, "Tune-in to the space you create when you're totally loving and accepting of yourself. See that you have the potential to do or have done the same thing as the person you feel separate from. Expand your own love and compassion to include them.

Practice! Practice!
◆◆◆◆◆◆◆◆◆◆◆◆◆◆

14

Choice Process

The choice process is a simple process that you can use any time to help yourself to open up choices and alternatives in your life. In doing it, you use your own creativity to find new ways to achieve your positive intention.

Your positive intention is ALWAYS available to you (the sun is always shining). It is just that sometimes we block our experience of it with clouds of addictions.

Using the Choice Process, you can take a giant step away from continuing a cycle of suffering and into creating the experience that you want.

Here are the three steps of the process:

1. Pinpoint your addiction: I create the experience of _____ because I choose to demand _____ .

2. My positive intention behind this addiction is to feel _____ (*or to see myself as* _____ .

3. Three new ways to achieve this positive intention are:

> (List three new ways: they can include specific Methods usage, any ways to change your perspective, and changing the outside world. IMPORTANT! THESE ARE NEW WAYS TO ACHIEVE YOUR POSITIVE INTENTION, **NOT** WAYS TO GET WHAT YOU ARE DEMANDING.)

Your own internal experience is the *only* thing you can always change. Therefore, in order to be successful with this process it is crucial that Step 2 relate to the internal experience you are seeking to establish through your demand. (How would you feel if you got your demand satisfied? How would you see yourself if you managed to get what you are demanding? One or the other - or both - of these answers will identify your positive intention.) Actually, the reason you are making that demand is *in order* to feel what you've identified in Step 2.

Notice that your addiction does not achieve your positive intention. Continuing to trigger the addiction just creates suffering! In Step 3, you take time to look for more skillful ways to create the internal experience that you want. Using the Methods can directly and skillfully help you to achieve the desired change in internal experience. Using the Methods may also help you to realize that you already have your positive intention met and that your addiction is just blocking you from realizing it.

Here are two examples of the choice process:

1. I create the experience of anger and resentment because I choose to demand that Henry not spend money on new carpeting.

2. My positive intention is to feel secure.

3. Three new ways to achieve that positive intention are:

--To see that Henry buying the carpet does not create my insecurity; only my programming does. (Link the Suffering with the Addiction).

--To look at what I *do* have and see that we do have enough money for what we need and that my fear and worry come from looking at my world from the security center (Centers of Consciousness).

--To ask for a raise, so that I have more money.

--Cut back on entertainment and miscellaneous expenses until the carpeting is paid off.

1. I create the experience of fear, panic and disappointment because I choose to demand that Al have called the Chicago office.

2. My positive intention is to feel relaxed.

3. Three new ways that I can achieve this positive intention:

--Say the fourth Pathway to myself and experience this situation with the programming of that Pathway: I always remember that I have everything I need to enjoy my here and now unless I am letting my consciousness be dominated by demands and expectations based on the dead past or the imagined future.

--Keep in my mind the reprogramming phrase: "I can feel calm and relaxed when Al didn't make the calls."

--Take a few deep breaths quickly, shake out tension and then relax totally for 10 minutes.

--Ask Al to give me a shoulder massage while he explains why he didn't make the call.

Achieving your positive intention is often more valuable than getting your demand satisfied! Let us suppose in this situation that Al *DID* make the call - only to get unwanted bad news. It might be difficult to feel relaxed - even though the original demand was satisfied! Achieving the positive intention puts YOU back in charge of your emotions, rather than being dependent on outside situations.

The value of the Choice Process is that we begin to acknowledge all the ways we can achieve our intentions and CHOOSE which way to bring that about. We are free from depending on our demands being satisfied to feel peaceful, happy or secure!

Let yourself be as creative as you can to think of new alternatives! There are ALWAYS ways to achieve your positive intention!

15

Sharing of Space (SOS)

Sharing of Space, or SOS, is a process created to assist us in sharing our separating feelings openly and honestly with others. Using the SOS process limits interference from our ego and helps us share without (1) blaming or (2) trying to get the other person to change. It's important to remember that the SOS is for you, not the person with whom you are sharing it. It is designed to enable you to break through barriers of separation you have created.

Here is the form used for Sharing of Space:

1. Begin by saying, "I want to feel closer to you by sharing an illusion I have created. I create the experience of_____ because I choose to demand_____."

2. Listen to the other person's response without interruption.

3. Feed back what the other person has said and get his/her acknowledgment that your summary is accurate. Give your feedback in the form, "I hear you say_____."

4. End by saying, "Thank you for being with me."

The SOS process utilizes the seventh, eighth and ninth Pathways. Optimally, you first use the ninth Pathway: "I act freely when I am tuned-in, centered and loving, but if possible I avoid acting when I am emotionally upset and depriving myself of the wisdom that flows from love and expanded consciousness."

This means you

USE ONE OR MORE LIVING LOVE METHODS

to uplevel your addictions to preferences or gain what insights you can in the situation. Using the Methods before you share helps you take more responsibility for creating your experience. Whatever the other person is doing or has done, you are responsible for creating your emotional reaction. The other person is simply "doing what he or she does," just being himself or herself. He or she is not "doing it to you."

You then use the seventh Pathway: "I open myself genuinely to all people by being willing to fully communicate my deepest feelings, since hiding in any degree keeps me stuck in my illusion of separateness from other people."

If you've used the Methods and you still are hanging on to your demand (which means the demand is still in your consciousness), then the next step in your growth is to share exactly and completely with those involved the feelings you have created. Remember, hiding separates—openness unites.

Share your feelings

One of the ways our egos keep us separate from others and from sharing what we really feel is having thoughts like: "the other person might get upset," "it'll cause more separation" and "I'll hurt them."

That's where you use the eighth Pathway: "I feel with loving compassion the problems of others without getting caught up emotionally in their predicaments that are offering them messages they need for their growth."

Using the eighth Pathway does not mean the other person will not react to your sharing. It means that if they do react, it will be from their own addictive programming—not what you have shared with them. No matter what you share, remember:

Addictions are the only immediate, practical cause of suffering

The SOS process is not designed to get other people to change. Nor is it designed to make you "feel better." It is designed to get out into the open all the stuff you keep hidden in your head because you tell yourself it's important or real or right or necessary or whatever. It helps you see just how unimportant it all is. When we keep anything hidden we are giving it an importance that is totally illusory. Hiding starts a chain of events.

We hide "IT" . . . "IT" must be important . . . If "IT" is important, we must protect "IT" . . . To protect "IT" we must keep others away . . . Separation is created. When we do this, we hurt ourselves more than anyone else could hurt us. Nothing is worth creating separation from other people.

Share

Rules of the game for SOS are:

Be totally honest   Share openly

Use the form exactly   Don't discuss the SOS

Be totally honest: If you are really angry and, while sharing, don't know if you want to feel closer to the other person, share that! If you are still hanging on to your addictive demand and you want the other person to change, share that. If you're blaming him/her and not wanting to take responsibility, share that. Be where you're at. Just be honest about it. Remember—that is the greatest gift you can give another person.

Use the form exactly: It means just that—exactly. Don't change it at all. If you do, you'll find your ego will get into the sharing and will start to defend itself. The process soon moves from a sharing to an argument.

Share openly: Don't hide. There is nothing you have to hide. The simplest way to realize that is to start sharing all the things you think you need to hide.

Don't discuss the SOS: Don't talk about anything that came up in the SOS process for at least 12 hours. While you might follow the form exactly and share openly and honestly, the minute you start talking about it, your ego starts trying to prove you're right. The other ego will defend and the sharing becomes an argument. Give you and the other person space to do your inner work before you share again.

Sharing is so important for us at the training center that we share not just our addictive spaces, but also our thoughts, opinions and all the things we don't want the other person to know. So much separation can be overcome in such a short period of time with just regular sharings. If you live with someone, work with someone daily or just value a relationship, share your "stuff" every day. Share openly and honestly.

BEING YOU—RIGHT WHERE YOU ARE—IS THE GREATEST GIFT YOU CAN GIVE ANOTHER PERSON

When you want to use the SOS process with someone who is not familiar with Living Love terminology, here's how you can retain the form and use alternative words:

SOS form	Same form—new words
1. I want to feel closer to you by sharing an illusion I create.	1. I haven't been feeling close to you lately. I'd like to talk about it.
2. I create the experience of (emotion) because I choose to demand (what you want).	2. I am feeling (emotion). I take responsibility for these feelings and I would like you to know that I want (state what you want).
3. Listen to the other person's response without interruption.	3. Listen to other person's response without interruption.
4. Feed back an accurate summary of his/her response. Get an acknowledgment that your summary is accurate.	4. Feed back an accurate summary of his/her response. Get an acknowledgment that your summary is accurate.
5. Say, "Thank you for being with me."	5. Say, "Thanks for letting me share with you."

Find the words that feel comfortable to you. Retain the form of the SOS process and share. All SOS rules still apply.

This is an example for using the SOS form with someone unfamiliar with Living Love terminology. The addictive demand is:

"I create the experience of annoyance because I choose to demand that you not chew your gum so noisily."

Remember, retain the form. Simply use different words.

1. "I find I've been avoiding you; I'd like to talk about it with you. I have been making myself feel annoyed when I hear you chewing your gum, because I don't want you to make so much noise. It's just a model I have in my head and really has nothing to do with you as a person."

2. "Oh, I'm sorry. I didn't realize I was so noisy. You should have told me sooner."

3. Feed back what he/she says. Remember to get the acknowledgment that your feedback is accurate. He/she might interrupt and add things while you are doing this. Simply feed back whatever he/she says, without adding any of your own opinions or getting defensive. "I just want to check that I've heard you correctly. I'm hearing you say that you're sorry; that you didn't realize you were so noisy; that I should have told you sooner."

4. "I appreciate this opportunity for us to share our feelings about this."

While this example may seem trite or silly, this is the exact type of thoughts we all refuse to share or even use the Methods with. These are addictions too!

Use the Methods
Share your feelings!

Regular use of the SOS process will deepen your honesty, your commitment and your level of inner work.

16

Summary

From the day we were born we have been developing, through our programming, a concept of who we are—picking up bits and pieces here and there, creating an idea of "self" in a rather disorganized, often chaotic, irrational and inconsistent fashion. We were guided in developing our idea of "self" by what seemed "workable" in the various situations we experienced as we grew.

The different possibilities of these constructed "selves" are endless: wealthy or poor, fat or thin, intellectual or non-intellectual, aggressive or submissive, sad or happy, angry or afraid. Add to that the unlimited variations made possible by combining any number of the above. And we will have many images or selves we think we are.

Which is the right "self"? Which is the better "self"? Well, such questions usually boil down to which "self" works here and now. It is our programming developed over the years that in each here-and-now moment determines what that "self" will be. And either consciously or unconsciously we make a choice between the following alternatives:

1. **Keep our present ideas of "self" intact and do everything possible to hold our outside world steady and unchanging [this usually means keeping the same people, same occupations, same landmarks, same roles handy].**

2. **Keep our present ideas of "self" intact and try to act differently in different situations. We act one way for this person and a different way for that person. We fake it and try to become skillful at our acting so no one will notice the difference.**

3. **Disassemble or let go of these ideas of "self" through consciousness growth or spiritual practice, so we intuitively choose the best course of action in each situation to produce love and oneness. Without this idea of "self" to protect or hide, we experience peace, lack of threat, a "home-like" comfort in each new here-and-now situation.**

Certainly we have all tried variations of the first two alternatives again and again. Most of us have begun to acknowledge the futility of such action to produce a life of love and happiness. We are now beginning to experiment with the third alternative. This is what the Living Love system or any other consciousness growth method can offer you.

We meet the challenge of letting go of our concepts of "self" with degrees of timidity, resolve, suspicion, hope, despair or whatever. And sometimes, after we begin disassembling or letting go of these ideas of ''self,'' we appear to run into brick walls. We are convinced, at least temporarily, that the process is not working, is working too slowly or is too threatening, and we will go back to alternatives one and two. Or we will settle for some variation of one, two and three.

After all, these concepts of ''self'' have taken on a life of their own. Our concepts of ''self'' have evolved from our programming and input from the world around us. It provides us with what appears to be, and even feels like, a complex living, breathing ''real'' entity. Now, that living, breathing ''real'' entity doesn't want to see itself disassembled. Would you? And wouldn't you do everything within your power to struggle for your own survival?

Sure, you might allow a few little alterations that appear to improve and enhance your ego image (like going to college or finishing school)—but to disappear entirely? Impossible! Why, that would be like death itself!

This battle between giving up or letting go of the programmed idea of ''self'' and the struggle to protect and guard this ''real'' living entity is the predicament we face. We need to develop a deep compassion for these ideas of ''self'' that we have identified with for so many years. This programming we have so zealously guarded, protected, enhanced and expanded is now, from its point of view, suddenly and unwittingly under attack.

Our ego-self has made a place in the world. It is admired and befriended by others, stands up for what it believes, does what is expected of it, laughs, cries, experiences the ups and downs of life, and now slowly, piece by piece, it is being evicted. And it will not stand for such ingratitude . . . such blasphemy.

And what would you do if faced with the same predicament? Talk your way out? Try to strike a bargain? Launch a counteroffensive? Hide? Wait for the right opportunity to sabotage the threat? Struggle to the finish, grasping at whatever straws were within reach? Go undercover, disguising yourself so that you are no longer recognizable? All of the above? More?

Any question why the consciousness growth game can be such a subtle, elusive, hair-raising, agonizing adventure? Any question why you sometimes feel stuck, discouraged, frustrated? Of course not! It's literally a game of life and death—at least to the programming we've been used to calling our ''self.''

So, what can we do? Simple—just enjoy the journey. Your strength lies in your determination to be free of programmed responses and reactions to the world outside of you. The consciousness growth practice you've chosen will work to uncover the peaceful you that enjoys increased perceptiveness, energy and love. All you have to do is stick with it.

Hear the outcries of the vanishing ''self''—explore them, investigate them and return to your practice. See the traps, the illusions, the warning signs, the frustrations, the fears, as a necessary part of the journey. Work to accept it all: the highs and lows. Because all you are really losing is your source of unhappiness.

All you have to do is practice with the Methods every day. Love yourself just exactly where you are.

There is no greater joy than the experience of discovering the real you behind the illusions of "self." You will find that the world has been set up to help you over the tough spots and speed you on your way. And as you lose the addictions that have held this concept of "self" so tightly together, so rigid, you will automatically develop the confidence that you need to take the next step.

Your life will take on a fluidity, a lightness, that will enable you to "enjoy it all." Not striving to change yourself or others. Not protecting. Not blaming. Not worrying about what the future might hold. You will experience an aliveness that you always have known existed. From deep within you will flow your own creative ability to live in a world characterized by wisdom, joy and love. After all, it is your birthright—and there is no reason to settle for less.

Using the Methods: a quick review

As you become aware of an addiction, all you need to do is simply:

1. Pinpoint your specific addiction:

I CREATE THE EXPERIENCE OF (separating emotions).

BECAUSE I CHOOSE TO DEMAND (specifically what you want).

2. Identify your positive intention

MY POSITIVE INTENTION BEHIND THIS DEMAND IS TO FEEL _____ .

(OR) TO SEE MYSELF AS _____ .

3. Use a Method.

THE TWELVE PATHWAYS

These are twelve statements containing wisdom that can guide you in any situation, can help you calm your mind and can be used as general reprogramming phrases. To use them:

—Say all twelve Pathways.
—Say one or more Pathways as many times as you choose.
—Say your positive intention and one Pathway alternately.
—Say your positive intention with each of the Pathways.
—Create your own way!

CENTERS OF CONSCIOUSNESS

This method can help you to gain perspective and see the choices you have to create your experience. To use it:

—Become aware of which centers of consciousness you are using; just name the center of consciousness you are in at any moment.
—Use your imagination and replay the scene through the security, sensation, power and love centers (and/or cornucopia and/or conscious-awareness).
—Use your imagination and replay the scene through the love and/or cornucopia and/or conscious-awareness centers.
—Create your own way.

LINK THE SUFFERING WITH THE ADDICTION

—Use any or all of these four steps:

1. Explore the suffering (ripoffs).

2. Pinpoint the specific addiction: I create the experience of _____
because I choose to demand _____ .

Look at "What is": I am emotionally resisting_____.

3. Make a choice:

Uplevel to a preference	Hold on to addiction
-Suffering stops	-Suffering continues
-You can more skillfully achieve your positive intention	-"What is" often remains the same
-You can maintain your opinion	-It interferes with achieving your true positive intention.
-You can still dislike "what is"	
-You can continue to change "what is"	

4. Become aware of the payoffs.

—Any way you make the connection that it is your addiction causing your suffering.

THE CATALYST—ALL WAYS US LIVING LOVE

Focus your mind on these words to help you calm your mind: All Ways Us Living Love. You can use the Catalyst when you are caught up, as a background for your day or for a specified period of time. To use it:

—Say it over and over.
—Say it and emphasize each successive word (ALL Ways Us Living Love, All WAYS Us Living Love, All Ways US Living Love, All Ways Us LIVING Love, All Ways Us Living LOVE.)
—Sing it.
—Create your own way to experience the Catalyst.
—Invent your own Catalyst.

CONSCIOUSNESS FOCUSING

With this Method you choose a phrase that contains loving, accepting programming and say it over and over to replace addictive programming with preferential programming. To use it, choose a reprogramming phrase. Then say that phrase over and over:

—Meditatively, quietly.
—With activity such as jogging or other physical exercise.
—As you go about your daily activities.
—Aloud or silently in your mind, tensing your body for increased intensity.
—Before going to sleep or when you wake up in the morning.
—When and how it feels right to you.

INSTANT CONSCIOUSNESS DOUBLER

Expanding your love and compassion by realizing the "us" place behind programming.

— Realizing that you have loved and accepted yourself when you said, did or thought the same thing as another person from whom you feel separate. Expand your compassion to include that person.

— Realizing that if you had the other person's programming, you would have said or done the exact same thing. Expand your compassion to include all of us trapped in our programming.

— Imagining the other person's possible positive intention. Realizing their actions are just unskillful attempts at achieving their true positive intentions.

— When you reject yourself, realizing that you would love and accept your best friend saying or doing the same thing. Expand that love and compassion to include yourself.

— Realizing that you have a very understandable positive intention. Feel compassion for yourself in the unskillful attempt you have made at achieving your true intention.

— Any way or any time you can put yourself in "their shoes."

17

Glossary

ADDICTION: An emotion-backed demand, desire, expectation or model that makes you upset or unhappy if it is not satisfied. It may be a demand on yourself, on another person or a situation.

ADDICTIVE DEMAND: Another term for addiction.

ADDICTIVE SNARL: Multiple and/or conflicting emotion-backed demands. Snarls are usually kept going by beliefs or unconscious assumptions that are generally hidden from your awareness.

ADDICTIVE TAPE: The words and phrases you have programmed that automatically run through your mind when you are feeling separating emotions.

BUILDING A CASE: Finding an increasing number of logic-tight reasons for making someone or something wrong and thus keeping you from emotionally accepting "what is." The crystallizing of the mind into a rock-like position that greatly limits your mental flexibility, practical give-and-take and willingness to work with a life situation.

BUYING INTO STUFF: When you emotionally identify with (or emotionally resist) another person's addictive models of how he/she, someone, something or you should be, and create separating feelings in yourself.

CAUGHT UP: Uptight. Feeling any separating emotions. Running addictive tapes.

CENTERED: The experience of feeling enough in yourself, with all other people and things seen neither as threatening nor as constituting a problem. Feeling calm, peaceful, aware, clear-minded, not caught in an addiction. When you are centered, you are able to tune-in to your inner wisdom.

CHANGING THE "OUTSIDE WORLD": Putting energy into changing situations or people (including yourself) that you wish to be different, as contrasted with doing the inner work of upleveling your addiction to a preference.

CLEAR: Having no addictive demands triggered; feeling completely accepting; not creating any separating emotions.

COP OUT: To consciously or unconsciously avoid acknowledging, looking at or working on a demand. To deal with an easier or safer issue rather than handling what is really bothering you or what is difficult for you to face.

COP TO: To share "stuff" you would normally hide; to admit; to be open and honest about.

EGO: The master controller of your mind that determines what is processed onto the screen of your consciousness. The ego is your friend, but it often operates from separating, addictive tapes and false-to-fact core beliefs. These create the illusory experience of the separate-self, whose domain of security, sensation and power is continually threatened by "what is." As you retire these separating tapes by working on your addictive programming, the ego activates tapes that let you experience the unified-self, which transforms your experience of yourself and of the world around you.

EGO-MIND: A compound term referring to the joint operations of the ego (when it selects which addictions are being threatened) and the rational mind (when it searches for solutions to protect the addictions by creating "me-vs.-them," "right-wrong" and "subject-object" thought forms). The ego-mind thereby continually maintains the illusion of the separate-self.

FEEDING AN ADDICTIVE DEMAND: Satisfying your addictive demand or model instead of using the Methods to uplevel it to a preference; using reprogramming phrases that reinforce your demand.

FLOW: When something follows without pushing or forcing.

GAME: An activity of life that has do's and don'ts and a win-loss position. "Game" refers to the roles we play in life, e.g., the marriage game, the parent game, the consciousness growth game, the insurance game, the sex game. This meaning of "game" should not be confused with the way in which it was used in **Games People Play** by Eric Berne, which refers to dishonest ploys that you use to manipulate another person. When we play life as a game, we can avoid the heaviness of a "right-wrong" judgmental approach and instead create an effective and enjoyable experience of life.

GROSS ADDICTION: An addiction that triggers definite emotions, such as anger, fear or frustration. (Also see Subtle Addiction, Niggle.)

ILLUSION: A distorted perception of "what is." The mind produces illusions to the degree that it is running addictions.

INNER WORK: The process of consciously using the Living Love Methods to gain insight, uplevel your addictions to preferences and love unconditionally.

LOVE: Emotional acceptance is both the goal of love and the means toward the goal. The experience of love is created when our perception is not being distorted by "me-vs.-them" perceptions. Love is the experience of others as "us" and not separately as "him," "her" or "them." Addictions are the enemy of love. Love increases when we handle our judgmentalness and feelings of separateness from ourselves and others.

LOVER: Someone who is not triggering addictive demands in you. You may create the same person to be a lover in one moment and your teacher in the next.

MELODRAMA: Your "act"; your actions on the stage of life. The purpose of this term is to help you experience the moment-to-moment events in your life as though it were a play or drama production. This helps you see your here and now in perspective and with detachment instead of creating threatening self-conscious addictive perceptions that keep pushing your emotional buttons.

MODEL: An expectation; a particular form or standard of how you, someone else or a situation "should be" or "shouldn't be." Models can be either preferential or addictive.

NIGGLE: An addictive demand with little emotional intensity. You may or may not be aware of a change in your feelings and body. Niggles can build up and keep you feeling separated and alienated.

OM: Sanskrit word; sound said to be the sum total of all energy. We use it to focus our energy and bring us together as a group.

PAYOFF: Some psychological, emotional or physical reward that can induce you to hold on to an addiction. Payoffs may be real or illusory.

POSITIVE INTENTION: The internal experience you really want in a particular situation, behind the surface demand or desire.

PREFERENCE: A desire that is not backed up with any separating emotions or tensions in the body. It's a preference if you do not create any separating emotions when you do not get what you want. You can put energy into making changes from a preferential space, but you are not attached to the results and remain loving of yourself and others. Preferences are experienced through the fourth, fifth and/or sixth centers of consciousness.

PROGRAMMING: Everything that we tell ourselves consciously or unconsciously. What we create our actions from.

RATIONAL MIND: The function of your brain that analyzes, justifies and is logical. It is activated by ego to protect security, sensation and power territories. Rational mind becomes your master when it is perpetuating a consciousness of separateness. Rational mind is also used to determine what is most workable when you have preferential programming.

"REAL YOU": Your conscious-awareness; your essence as a human being as distinguished from the changing process of your body, mind, emotions, thoughts, social roles or actions.

RIP-OFF: A way in which holding on to a demand keeps you from feeling loving, being effective and enjoying your life. Your suffering and unhappiness. Getting less than is available; negatively affecting, e.g., "rip-off energy."

ROLLER-COASTERING: The up-and-down experience of feeling good when your addictions are satisfied and feeling afraid, frustrated, angry, etc. when life is not meeting your addictive demands. The oscillation between addictive highs and addictive lows.

SEPARATE-SELF: The illusory "me-vs.-them" perceptions that guard your security, sensation and power addictions. The mental programs that create the experience of one's life as a battle against oneself, other people and the world instead of the compassionate, understanding and wise flowing of energy through the unified-self that sees how it all fits into a common pattern of individual and social growth and enjoyment.

SEPARATING EMOTIONS: Feelings, such as fear, disappointment, anger, hurt boredom, loneliness, guilt, unhappiness, that create the illusion of alienation from yourself and/or other people.

S/HE: To be read as "she or he."

SOAP OPERA: See "melodrama." The "games" of life being played out on the stage of the world. The term is helpful in reminding us to take lightly what's happening and not get caught up in seriousness.

STUFF: Separating emotions such as fear, frustration and anger. The chains of rationalizing, criticizing, judging and blaming thoughts and actions that are triggered by one's addictions. (Also see "Buying Into Stuff.")

SUBJECT-OBJECT: Experiencing yourself as all-important and viewing others as pawns that help you get something you want in life—or avoid something you don't want. Subject-object refers to seeing yourself as subject and others as objects which either enhance or threaten your self-image. Not relating to people as human beings like yourself.

SUFFERING: The unconscious or conscious experience of any separating feeling in any degree; when suffering is continual, you experience unhappiness.

TAPE: Your verbal, emotional and bodily responses to life situations. Words that go through your mind; programming in your biocomputer. Tapes may be preferential or addictive.

TEACHER: A person, situation or object that puts us in touch with our addictive programming. Consciousness growth requires that we open ourselves to the "teachings" that occur in the daily interactions of life.

TUNNEL VISION: Viewing "what is" from a narrow perspective so that only a few elements are seen and are thus blown up in importance. Being blind to most aspects of a situation.

TUNE-IN TO: Become aware of; listen to; explore or experience.

UNIFIED-SELF: "Us" instead of "me-vs.-them" programming. Programming that gives us an overall perspective of how everything fits perfectly into our journey through life, either for our growth or our enjoyment. The unified-self thus creates an experience of people and situations as a unified or integral part of our journey instead of a nuisance or threat.

"WHAT IS": What you are choosing to addictively resist (which may be a real or imagined situation). "What is" also refers to impartial, objective reality; the way the universe is unfolding as contrasted with the illusory versions you create by your addictive demands.

WINS: Insights into ways by which you are getting freer of your addictive programming.

18

Living Love

Songs

Records and tape cassettes (in stereo) of Living Love music albums are available by mail order from Living Love Publications. Write Living Love Publications, 790 Commercial Avenue, Coos Bay, Oregon 97420 for information and prices.

The Oneness Space

I JUST GO ON LOVIN' YOU
by Summer Raven (©1975)
Vocals—Cloudia, with Mary Carol

I know sometimes it's hard for you
To let yourself be free,
'Cause I can feel the struggle
Deep inside of you (oh yeah!)
I know that I can't change your life
It's up to you to be
What you feel
Is really you (oh yeah!)

Chorus:
No matter what you say or what you do
I know my love will see me through
And I just go on lovin' you
Yes I do!
I just go on loving you.

I can see how you might think
I want something from you,
But I don't want to take
What you can't give me (oh no!)
I'm here to learn from what we are
And what we try to do.
Just be yourself my friend
And you help me be free.

Chorus

I'm so close to what you are
'Cause you're so much like me.
I guess that's why I love
To watch the things you do (oh yeah!)
And I find I love myself
When I'm loving you.
I'm just your face in the mirror
Laughing back at you (oh yeah!)

I TAKE RESPONSIBILITY
by Summer Raven (©1975)
Vocals—Summer, with Cassandra

Chorus:
I take responsibility
For the way I feel
'Cause I create the experience
That I take as real.

When I feel myself gettin' uptight—
And I tell myself the world ain't right—
And I can see I'm headed for a fight
—I'm headed for a fight—

Chorus

When I find that I'm afraid of you—
And I'm scared of what you might do—
And I'm feelin' mighty helpless too
—I'm feelin' helpless, too—

Chorus

When it's pleasure I'm lookin' for
And I feel that my life is a bore
There's not enough and I gotta have more
—I just gotta have more—

Chorus

Now I know that no one's to blame
For the feelings I get in life's game
I'm the one who creates the pain
—Who creates the pain—

THERE IS ONLY ONE
by Summer Raven © 1975
Vocals—Buckie, with Marcus
and Sue Ann

I am a humble servant,
A part of one great plan.
I'm here to love and serve you
In every way I can.
I am a holy vessel
Full to overflowing.
I give to all who ask of me
And care not where I'm going.

Chorus:
Pure light shines through me.
My task has just begun—
Now that I can see
There is only one.

I am the Royal Master
And Ruler of my soul.
All I need will come to me—
There's nothing to control.
I am an inspiration
Here for all to see.
I share my life with everyone
And know in truth I'm free.

Chorus

**NOTHING'S MORE IMPORTANT THAN
THE ONENESS SPACE**
by Summer Raven (©1975)
Vocals—Sue Ann and Cassandra,
with Rita and Marcus

Chorus:
Nothing's more important than the oneness
space.
It comes from your heart. It's a happy place.
Love can put a smile on your face
And give you so much more!

It lets you see and it sets you free.
It gives you so much energy.
Love can end your misery
And open any door!

Chorus

Love can give you peace of mind.
Love can teach you to be kind.
Love's the perfect way to find
What you're lookin' for!

Chorus

Love is the sparkle in your eye.
Love will always get you high.
Love's the smoothest way to fly—
Feel your spirit soar!

Chorus

**BEWARE WHAT YOU
TELL YOURSELF**
by Summer Raven (©1975)
Vocals—'The Angels':
Sue Ann, Rita, Cassandra

Beware what you tell yourself,
Children of light.
Demanding and judging
Will alter your sight.
And forcing your way
Always leads to a fight,
'Cause nothing is wrong
More than anything's right.

Wherever you wander,
Don't leave love behind!
Whatever you're giving
Is what you will find.
Accept what life shows you
Or live like the blind—
The beauty or ugliness
Comes from your mind.

When life didn't please us
We made ourselves sad.
When we couldn't control things
We made ourselves mad.
This kept us from loving
What we already had,
What we want we call good,
What we don't we call bad.

Remember our spirit
And follow your heart.
We can make our own troubles
Or take them apart.
When the tragedy ends,
Watch the comedy start.
In the story of life
You're just playing your part.

THAT'S THE WAY IT IS BY GOLLY
by Summer Raven (©1975)
Vocals—Summer, with everybody else

When the sun don't shine on Monday,
I don't wish that it was Sunday
I just smile and shrug my shoulders,
That's the way it is.
Chorus:
That's the way it is, by golly
That's the way it is, by golly
That's the way it is, by golly
That's the way it is.

People come and people go
Some say yes and some say no
I just smile and shrug my shoulders,
That's the way it is.

Chorus

Life is like a merry-go-round
Sometimes up and sometimes down
I just smile and shrug my shoulders,
That's the way it is.

Chorus

We can laugh and we can cry,
First we're born and then we die
I just smile and shrug my shoulders,
That's the way it is.

Chorus

When my mother tells me no
I don't tell her where to go
I just smile and shrug my shoulders,
That's the way it is.

Chorus

When I come home from a date
And Mom gets mad and says I'm late
I just smile and shrug my shoulders,
That's the way it is.

Chorus

When I'm smokin' in my room
And my Dad yells with the voice of doom
I just smile and shrug my shoulders,
That's the way it is.

Chorus

When I'm feelin' sad and lonely
'Cause I don't have my one and only
I just smile and shrug my shoulders,
That's the way it is.

Chorus

When I spend the whole day cookin'
And it burns when I'm not lookin'
I just smile and shrug my shoulders,
That's the way it is.

Chorus

When I slave for every penny
And my wife won't save us any
I just smile and shrug my shoulders,
That's the way it is.

Chorus

When my grandson and I can't rap
I don't blame it on the generation gap
I just smile and shrug my shoulders,
That's the way it is.

Chorus

When anything in my life goes wrong
I just sing this simple song
I just smile and shrug my shoulders,
That's the way it is.

I CAN SURRENDER
by Summer Raven (©1975)
Vocals—Susan and Sue Ann

Chorus:
I can love everything
I can feel, I can see
I can hear my heart sing
I can love to be me.

I can surrender
And long for no more
When I think life should give me
What life gave me before.

I can surrender
And let myself be.
Like the birds and the flowers
I too can be free.

Chorus

I can surrender
To sorrow and pain
Do the birds fight the seasons?
Do flowers fight rain?

I can surrender
To pleasure and bliss,
And treasure each moment
That gives me all this.

Chorus

EVERYONE'S BEEN BLUE
by Summer Raven (©1975)
Vocals—Susan, with Sue Ann
and Marcus

Chorus:
It's OK to be unhappy, honey,
Everyone's been blue, and
Blue's a pretty color, baby,
When it's worn by you.
It's OK to lose your way, my love,
We've all been lonely too.
It's OK to be the way you are—
No matter what you do!

We thought when we were children
We could always make a deal
At a game called "pleasing others"—
Learned which feelings to conceal.
Sure would like to see you happy
But your sorrow's just as real,
And you can learn to love yourself
No matter what you feel!

Chorus

I know it kinda scares you
When you feel your spirit sink.
Just hang on to this chain of hope—
There's love in every link.
You know I used to be so low myself—
I drove myself to drink.
Now I'm learning to accept myself
No matter what I think!

Chorus

THE WHOLE WIDE WORLD'S MY HOME
by Summer Raven (©1975)
Vocals—Cassandra, with Rita and Sue Ann

Chorus:
No matter where I wander,
No matter where I roam,
I play my part with a happy heart.
The whole wide world's my home.

I started on my journey
The first time I took a breath,
The trail will end when I join my friend—
The one we all call death.

Chorus

I'm not afraid of hard times.
I can bounce back when I fall.
High or low, anywhere I go,
I've come to love it all.

Chorus

The future lies before me
Like an offer—not a vow.
The past is dead like a book I've read—
I'm living here and now.

Chorus

I watch my life unfolding.
I give my heart the lead.
I watch the show, cause now I know
I've got everything I need.

Chorus

'TIS THE GIFT TO BE SIMPLE
Old Shaker Song
Vocals—Sue Ann and Rita

'Tis the gift to be simple,
'Tis the gift to be free,
'Tis the gift to come down
where we ought to be,
And when we find ourselves
in the place just right
It will be in the valley
of love and delight.
When true simplicity is gained
To bow and to bend
we will not be ashamed.
To turn, to turn
it will be our delight
'Til by turning and turning
we come round right!

SWEET SURRENDER [TANTRIC VISION]
by Marcus (©1975 Mark Allen)
Vocals—Marcus

Teach me, O teach me
 Sweet surrender
May I learn, really learn to
 Love it all!
There is nothing to reject,
 there is beauty and wonder
 in each eternal moment
 here and now

I pray to deeply understand
 Sweet surrender
May I have the wisdom, now
To know what things can change,
 and have the strength to change them
 and to see what things cannot change
 and let them flow

May I forever know
 Sweet surrender
May I learn what it means
 to be free, to be free
May I live in love,
 may I remember
 everything has its beauty
 but not everyone can see

I pray to deeply understand
 Sweet surrender
I pray to have the heart and eyes to see
That good and bad, and right and wrong,
 and pain and bliss, and all
 are all branches of the same tree
They're all One in their real identity

Repeat first verse

Ocean of Love

OCEAN OF LOVE
by Marcus (©1975 Mark Allen)
Vocals—Susan Madley

She sings, she sings so sweetly
   She sings of love
The light, the light shining in her eyes
   Colors and spirits above
And she shows us, she shows us what love is—
   Light within your heart
Love is in every one of us
   Right within your heart
     Is an ocean of love
      Ocean of love
      Ocean of love
      Ocean of love

She speaks, she speaks so sweetly
   Of wondrous things
Shining with the light and love
   Sweet inspiration brings
Showing us, showing us how to love
   Without hanging on
Loving every moment
   Of life's ever-changing song
     In an ocean of love
      Ocean of love
      Ocean of love
      Ocean of love
      Ocean of love

May you be eternally loaded on love
May you fly forever high on the wings of a dove
May your heart be open for all time to everyone
May your love light shine on all
   Like the moon and the sun
     On an ocean of love
      Ocean of love
      Ocean of love

LOVE CENTER
by Marcus (©1975 Mark Allen)
Vocals—Marcus and everybody

Chorus:
Love Center, Love Center
Open up your heart,
Open up your heart

It's so easy to start
(Love Center)
Just feel your heart
(Love Center)
Open up your heart,
Open up your heart

All answers are there
(Love Center)
Everything is clear
(Love Center)
Open up your heart,
Open up your heart

Fill your body with light
(Love Center)
Let your love shine bright
(Love Center)
Open up your heart,
Open up your heart

Bridge:
Love shines from your heart,
Shinin' on us all so bright
We are never apart,
We are pure light
We are pure light!

Chorus

Next thing you know
(Love Center)
That light starts to grow
(Love Center)
Open up your heart,
Open up your heart

Repeat from bridge

**YOU GOT EVERYTHING YOU
NEED [RIGHT HERE AND NOW]**
by Marcus (©1975 Mark Allen)
Vocals—Cloudia and Marcus,
   with Sue Ann and Noj and Peter

You got everything you need
right here and now, O yeah
You got everything you need
right here and now, O yeah
But if you think that your happiness
   is somewhere else
Brothers and sisters, take a look
   at yourself
You got everything you need
right here and now, O yeah!

You got everything you need. . .
You may be fat and you
   may be thin
But you're just perfect
   in the shape you're in
You got everything you need
right here and now, O yeah

You got everything you need. . .
But if you think that your happiness
   is over the fence
Turn that addiction
   to a preference
You got everything you need
right here and now, O yeah

You got everything you need. . .
You may be black, brown, red,
   yellow, blue or white
Any way you are
   is outa sight!
You got everything you need
right here and now, O yeah

You got everything you need. . .
But if you're uptight or burned out
   or scrambled or fried
People take a look at
   the other side:
You got everything you need
right here and now, O yeah
You got everything you need
right here and now, O yeah!

ALL WE NEED IS LOVE
by Marcus (©1975 Mark Allen)
Vocals—Susan Madley and Joe Williams

Love is the answer,
   Love is the key
It can open any door,
   Give us eyes to see
In our hearts lies a secret,
   And it sets us free:
   All we need is love
   All we need is love.

Repeat

LET IT GO
by Summer Raven (©1976)

Chorus:
Let it go—let it go
And watch your life flow.
Don't let the good life pass you by.
Let it go—let it go
It's the only way I know
To find love, peace and happiness
   and rainbows in the sky.

Don't hang on to your problems,
Don't hang on to your tears
Lift up your heart with laughter,
Now let go of all your fears.
Where's the "happy ever after"
You've waited for all these years?
The answer's locked inside your heart
A prisoner of your fears.

Chorus

Don't hang on to your anger,
Don't hang on to your pain.
Let your heart be like sunlight
After a summer's rain.
Don't tell yourself you're sorry
That you've lived your life in vain.
Just give your life what you've got—
The more you give—the more you gain!
Don't hang on to life's pleasures
Or the things you think you need.
Tune-in to what you've got right now—
Life gives you what you need.
Don't let yourself be trapped,
By worry or by greed.
When you enjoy each moment,
You'll know that you've been freed!

Chorus

LIVING LOVE IS HOW I START
by Summer Raven (©1975)
Vocals—Susan Madley, with Sue Ann
   and Marcus

It was just a week ago
I let my true self know
I'm ready to receive your love.
Unite me with your light
Dancin' on a sunbeam burnin' bright.
Make me one with the shinin' sun above.
Living Love is how I start,
And sharin' all the secrets I keep
Deep down in my heart.

I spent such a lonely time
Puttin' all my sorrows into rhyme,
Runnin' from a monster I call Fear.
Now you're telling me, I know
I got no place to go
'Cause everything I need I got right here.
Living Love is how I start
And sharin' all the secrets I keep
Deep down in my heart.

I don't have to be afraid
Of all the monsters I have made
I'll tame them with my love—I'm learning how.
No matter where I roam,
I'm always safe at home
When I can be in heaven here and now.
Living Love is how I start,
And sharin' all the secrets I keep
Deep down in my heart.

I used to think my role
Was more important than my soul.
I used to think I needed lots of stuff.
Now I'm content to be
Like the ever-changing sea—
I'm happy being me
'Cause I'm enough!
Living Love is how I start,
And sharin' all the secrets I keep
Deep down in my heart.

Repeat last three lines

ACCEPT IT
by Marcus (©1975 Mark Allen)
Vocals—Sue Ann and Marcus,
   with Peter and Noj

Chorus:
Well, there's nothin' to do
   but accept it.
It don't do no good
   to reject it.
There's nothin' to do
   but accept it.
That's what is, that's what is
   let it flow on
   let it flow on
   let it flow on . . .

Whatever may be happening
   in your life—
It may be filled with pain,
   or fear, or strife—
When things seem just as bad
   as they can be,
Sweet brothers and sisters,
   here's a key:

Chorus

Change is the name of the game,
   my friend,
Things never stay the same,
   my friend,
There's just one choice
   we've got—ain't it so?
We can reject it,
   and fight it,
   or we can let it flow.

Chorus

Love is the key
   of which we sing—
To love and to accept
   are the same thing—
Just beyond all those words
   in your rational mind
Is an ocean of love
   and it's so easy to find:

Chorus

NOW I GATHER MY WINGS
by Summer Raven (©1975)
Vocals—Cloudia

I don't need his love to feel free
I've got all I need, loving me
And if he should enter my heart
There's no need to tear it apart.

Chorus:
Now I gather my wings
And heed the call of the skies.
Hear the raven! She sings!
Songs of love as she flies.

In eternity we are one.
Our love light shines like the sun.
In surrender we'll know the way
To love our lives every day.

Chorus

IT'S OK TO BE ME
by Summer Raven (©1975)
Vocals—Cloudia

It's OK to be me,
All alone and in pain,
Sittin' under a tree
At night in the rain—
I'm just doin' my thing
And it's my time to spend
And it's OK by me
I'm my own best friend.

Well the river don't worry
And the seasons don't care
Not one of these trees
Wants to go anywhere
It's only a movie
And I'm playin' my part
And right now this scene
Is a pain in my heart.

It's OK to be me
When I'm tryin' too hard
And I've lost all my money
And I've played my last card
I can't hang on to something
That I never had
And whatever I do
I don't call myself bad.

'Cause a person's a person
Whatever they do
I can let myself be
If I let you be, too—
It's just our illusions
That keep us apart
I know that we're friends
When I open my heart.

I'M GETTIN' FREE
by Summer Raven (©1975)
Vocals—Susan, with Martha

I'm gettin' free of all the fears
That make me feel so lost and lonely.
I don't have to be afraid
Of what the world will do to me!
I'm learning how to love
And love is stronger than my fears can be.
I'm learning how to love my life
I'm learning to be free!

I'm gettin' free of all the craving
That nearly drives me mad.
I don't ever have to feel that I need
Just what I don't have!
I'm learning how to love
And love will always satisfy me.
I'm learning how to love my life—
I'm learning to be free!

I'm gettin' free of all demanding
To have things my own way.
I don't have to control you
It's not worth the price I pay!
I'm learning how to love—
I don't have to force my way.
I'm learning how to love my life
More and more each day!

Repeat first verse

Open Up Your Vision

Written, arranged and produced by Jai Michael Jose
Vocals by Susan Madley, Stephen Fiske, Juniper L'Orange
Jai; All songs—words and music—©1979 Jai Michael Josefs

I'M THE ONE THAT I'VE BEEN LOOKING FOR

Vocals—Susan and Juniper

I've played the game of win and lose.
I've played the game of pick and choose.
I've played the game of making my baby cry.
I've played the game of broken heart.
I've played the game of brand new start.
But now there's one more game I'd like to try.

CHORUS:
I don't have to wear a frown
When my baby won't come 'round.
I don't have to play the games I played before.
I don't have to be uptight
If I'm not with somebody tonight
'Cause I'm the one that I've been looking for,
Oh yeah,
I'm enough and there's no need for more.

I've played the game of being alone,
Sitting by the telephone,
Looking for a number to call
that'd make me feel good.
I've played the game of running around
With every lover that I found.
But, somehow, none of them loved me
like I thought they should.

CHORUS

I've played the game of hiding my fears.
I've played the game of crying my tears.
I've played the game of wanting things
my own way.
I've played the game of being cool.
I've played the game of holding on like a fool.
But now I've found the key to making love
stay in my life.

CHORUS

PLAYIN' THE MONEY GAME
Vocals—Jai

Now since I opened up my heart
my whole life has been changed,
But I still go to work like anyone.
But now instead of wasting myself
chasing after cash,
I play the money game and I have fun.

CHORUS:
Playin' the money game
Playin' the money game
I am not addicted to power,
wealth or fame, no I'm just
Playin' the money game
Playin' the money game
Whether I win or lose I feel the same.

Now I used to make myself upset
with others on the job
Or only do enough to just get by.
But when I see each moment
as a chance to love and serve
Any work I do can get me high.

CHORUS

I used to think I needed fancy cars
and fancy clothes
To show the world my life
was working fine.
But now I don't need fancy things
to validate my life,
Cause all the love I need's already mine.

CHORUS

I LOVE YOU

Vocals—Juniper

I love you
Not just for what you mean to me
For the beautiful jewel you are
A flower in a field of joy
Whether you feel the love
inside yourself or not
I know it's there and I don't care
What tomorrow may find
My love for you is beyond time.

I love you
Behind the drama of our lives
Behind the passion that we feel
Behind the fears we think are real
Behind the storms I see
the rainbow in your heart
I feel the boundaries of our love
Reach far beyond the sky
My love for you can never die.
I love you.

I'LL WORK ON ME

Vocals—Stephen and Susan

Darling you know I love you,
But livin' with you everyday,
There's times I feel so mad
I just want to shout.
I put myself above you,
And tell you how you should be.
But there's a better way for us
to work it out.

CHORUS:
I'll work on me,
And you work on you.
That's the only way I know
To keep love shining through, and
I'll keep working on me
No matter what you do,
'Cause I don't ever
Want to stop loving you.

Sometimes I think you're crazy
Puttin' the blame on me,
When nothing's going like you want
it to go.
Sometimes I get so lazy
And just want you to change,
But that kind of change is never
going to help me grow.

CHORUS

Sometimes you start crying
About all the hurt you feel,
And I feel sad when I see you
in distress.
And there is no denying,
I'd rather see you smile,
But I can't bring you joy and happiness.

CHORUS

I know it would be easy,
If we got really free,
To spend all of my days
being lovers with you.
And that would really please me,
But until then, when we're down,
I'm going to let you be my teacher, too.

CHORUS

THE KEY TO UNDERSTANDING

Vocals—Juniper and Stephen

Today the time has come
to go our separate ways
But we don't have to say goodbye.
I love you now as much
as I did yesterday,
That part of us will never die.
It's clear to both of us
we need more space to grow,
For life goes on and
nothing stays the same.
And we can make ourselves
feel separate and sad,
Or live in love
and see it as a game.

CHORUS:
Well it's the key to understanding
And opening up your heart,
When you love me and I love you
We can each just play our part.
And it's the way to stop demanding
And find true happiness,
When I love me and you love you
There's no more loneliness.
(Repeat last two lines.)

I see us feeling sad
about the pain we shared
And worried we won't make it
on our own.
But I also see quite clearly
how strong we really are
And in our years together
how we've grown.
Don't fear the future
or cry about the past,
Right here and now
we both are free
To live each moment
in harmony and love
With everything we do and see.

CHORUS

DOIN' THE DANCE FROM LOVE

Vocals—Susan

It happened just a week ago
My lover wasn't around
When he was supposed to pick me up
On the other side of town.
But I didn't put him out of my heart
I hopped right on a bus
'Cause the only place I need to be
Is the place where we are us.

CHORUS:
Doin' the dance from love
Doin' the dance from love
You can flow with anything
When you're doin' the dance from love.

I worked all morning yesterday
I was really going strong
When my supervisor told me
That he'd started me out wrong.
So I did it all over again
And didn't get uptight
'Cause bein' in love means more to me
Than bein' in the right.

CHORUS

Now any time I get caught up
Around what people do
I sing myself this simple song
And it helps pull me through.
'Cause I know deep inside my heart
No matter what is said
The only thing I can really change
Is what's inside my head.

Chorus

'Cause behind all that
Here we are
Lovers on planet earth.
Behind all that
Here we are
Lovers on planet earth.
And we're just—
Doin' the dance from love
Doin' the dance from love
You can flow with anything
When you're doin' the dance from love.

LET IT OUT/LET IT IN
Vocals—Stephen and Susan

Chorus:
Let it out. (Let it out.)
Let it out. (Let it out.)
Don't hold back.
That's the way the change begins.
Let it out. (Let it out.)
Let it out. (Let it out.)
Don't hold back.
'Cause when you share the secret part
You open up your heart
  to let love in.
(Let it in.) Let it in. (Let it in.)

When you're feeling hurt and lonely
You think you've got no place to go
You lock your sorrow up inside your heart
'Cause you couldn't bear for anyone to know.
And what really makes it seem so bad
Is the fear that you're alone
But when you open up and let them out,
You'll find your fears
  are just like everyone's.

Chorus

When things don't go like
  you think they should,
Deep inside you get so mad.
But you bite your tongue and hold it back
'Cause you tell yourself
  that feeling rage is bad.
So you shut out everybody
And tell yourself that they don't care,
And all that does is make you angrier
But if you're looking for the way out
  just open up and share.

Chorus

LIVING YOUR LIFE IN LOVE
Vocals—Susan

Goin' to work in the morning
Used to be such a bore.
Wondering what it's for,
And why you go on.
Now you know there's a better way
To see the job that you do every day,
Doing service is the game that you play
When you're living your life in love.

Chorus:
Oh - Oh - Oh Get on your mark
  Ready to start
  Living your life in love.
    Repeat

Hanging out with your lover
Used to feel incomplete
When they refused to meet
The models you had.
Now you don't make yourself feel tense
'Cause the model's just a preference
And changing others doesn't make any sense
When you're living your life in love.

Chorus

Flyin' off of the handle
When somebody puts you down,
Greeting them with a frown
The next time you met.
Now there's no animosity
'Cause you don't take it personally,
You can love them unconditionally
When you're living your life in love.

Chorus

Making yourself feel embarrassed
When others would criticize
Watching confusion rise
And getting uptight.
Now you don't make yourself feel blue
'Cause you know that whatever you do,
Behind your script there's a perfect you
Living your life in love.

Chorus

THE ADDICTION SONG
Vocals—Susan

Now when your boss looks over your shoulder
With a cold, disapproving eye
And he says you're wrong and you better
Shape up, 'cause you got no alibi.
If you're feeling afraid
  when he's yelling at you
And go off by yourself to pout,

Chorus:
Then you know you've got an addiction
And it's time to start clearing it out.
Yes, you know you've got an addiction
And Sister (Brother) there ain't no doubt.
When you feel like you could die
If you don't get what you crave
And your emotional demands they
Make you feel like a slave,
You know you've got an addiction
And it's time to start clearing it out.
(3rd time only)
With Living Love. It's time to start
  clearing, clearing it out.

Now when you've already got your stereo
And your second color T.V.
But your best friend just bought
  a brand new car
And you're full of jealousy.
If you're getting so bored with the
  stuff that you have
And you're wondering what it's
  all about,

Chorus

Now when your life is rolling along
You're doin' what you like to do,
And suddenly everything
  seems to go wrong
Addiction's caught up with you.

Now when you come home to your honey
And you want to go out for some fun,
But he wants to talk about money
And won't let you leave til he's done.
If you try talking to him
  but you get uptight
Until you're angry enough to shout,

Chorus

DOIN' IT
Vocals—Jai

Well, there's no guru on the planet
Who'll completely put you through,
All they can do is point the way
The rest is up to you.
And there ain't no magic nowhere
Gonna open up your heart.
And a helpful book or teacher
Will only take you there in part.
But if you want to go all the way
Do your practices every day.
You know, you've got to be doin' it.

Now your mind wants to find a shortcut
For helping you to live each day
So you keep on shopping around, yeah,
Searching for a better way.
But every time you find a method
That you think is going to get you high.
Your ego won't let you stay with it
And you go looking for another to try.
But if you want to go all the way
Do your practices every day.
You know, you've got to be doin' it.

Now some of us have found a teaching
To help us free our soul
And we're mighty glad we have the tools
To take us to our goal.
But sometimes every one of us
Needs a cosmic shove.
'Cause if we were supposed
  to just talk about it,
It wouldn't be called **living** love.
And if you want to go all the way
Do your practices every day.
You know, you've got to be

(Doin' it)
Recite the Pathways every day
(Doin' it)
SOS when you've got something to say
(Doin' it)
Every night do your Gettin' Free
(Doin' it)
And when you're caught up do an EIP

'Cause if you want to go all the way
Do your practices every day,
You know, you've got to be doin' it . . .
    Repeat

OPEN UP YOUR VISION
Vocals—Stephen and The Choir

When you wake up in the morning
And it's raining in your heart,
And you feel like you won't make it
Before you even start,
When your world is wrapped in darkness
And you cannot see the light
'Cause all your situations
Haven't seemed to work out right.
Open up your vision
And look past the reasons why
And open up your curtains
See the sun there in the sky.
Know that it's been shining
Even through the cloudy days,
And feel it's warmth inside you
As you sing this simple phrase:

"There is nothing to need,
  hide from, or fear
I am whole and complete,
  right now and right here."
    Repeat 4 times.
"There is nothing to need,
  hide from, or fear
We are whole and complete,
  right now and right here."
    Repeat 8 times

Carry the Love

LOVING ME IS ALL I HAVE TO DO
By Haven

When I feel lost and all alone
And scared and sad and blue
I sit and think of things I've done
And things I've tried to do

It doesn't really matter,
Things are as they should be
If I could just remember that . . .

Loving me is all I have to do,
Loving me is all I have to do

There came a time in my life
When everything went wrong
And angry thoughts ran through
My mind trying to take me along
It's just another feeling
So I'll turn it into love
And I'll give to you remembering

Loving me is all I have to do,
Loving me is all I have to do

It's time to see
Who I should be
There's time to find the answer
Go up and down
Then turn around
And recognize the dancer oh oh . . .

It seems as though I've tried to say
In many different ways
And all you do is see the image
That my words portray

And now that my reflection
Has turned around to you
I realize with special wonder that

Loving me is all I have to do,
Loving me is all I have to do
Loving me is all I have to do,
Loving me is all I have to do
Loving me is all I have to do.

BE THE ONE
Words and music by Tom Dalton

When you gonna live your life now
The way you always wanted to
When you gonna find the love that's
Deep inside of you

When you gonna climb the mountains
That lie across your path now
When you gonna be the one
You never quite allowed yourself to be
Be the one you want to be

When you gonna learn the lessons
That life is always giving
When you gonna cross the threshold
That makes life worth the living

When you gonna love somebody
The way you always wanted to
When you gonna find the love
It's all inside of you

And be, be the one you want to be
Be the one you want to be
Be the one
When you gonna change the patterns
That keep your life from growing
When you gonna free your spirit
And let your love start flowing

When you gonna let your light shine
Through all your fears and sorrow.
When you gonna claim your birthright
And be the one you want to be
Be the one you want to be

When you gonna love somebody
The way you always wanted to
When you gonna find the love
It's all inside of you

And be, be the one you want to be
Be the one you want to be (Repeat 2
times)

COMPASSION
Words and music by Tom Dalton

Some days the sun don't shine
Sometimes you lose that light
in your eyes
Some days you feel so low
Sometimes that feeling won't let go

Chorus

You can learn to carry on
You can learn that you are what you are
Don't you know that you're enough?
All you have to do is let yourself love

When you think somebody lets you down
And you can't seem to find
your way around
Look inside your heart to see
They are only doing what they feel

Bridge

Compassion is the key
Love is all you need
Compassion is the key
Love is all you need to be free

Everybody's not the same
Everybody plays a different game
Some will turn and walk away
Everyone must find their own way.

Chorus

Bridge

CARRY THE LOVE
By Haven

We are one incredible family
We are one incredible family
We are learning to live together
We are learning to love one another
We can be just who we are
We can be we can be
One incredible family

Time will take us where we go
And love will show us what to do
Laugh together play together
Share each other's rainbows
Carry the love, carry the love
We can be just who we are
We can be we can be
One incredible family
One incredible family

There's a place to learn Cornucopia
Where we all are loved Cornucopia
Children teach us sweet surrender
Life is just one moment here and now
Carry the love
We can be just who we are
We can be we can be
one incredible family (Repeat 3 times)
Carry the love (Repeat 3 times)

WHEN I OPENED UP MY HEART
Words and music by Tom Dalton

When I opened up my heart,
I opened up the door
When I opened up my heart,
I opened up the door
Everything is waiting inside,
Everything is waiting inside
All I did was open up my heart

When I give my love away,
I always get it back
When I give my love away,
I always get it back
All the love is waiting inside,
All the love is waiting inside
All I did was give my love away

When I bid my fears goodby,
My love starts to shine
When I bid my fears goodby,
My love starts to shine
Love is always shining inside,
Love is always shining inside
All I did was bid my fears goodby

When I let my feelings show,
My love starts to grow
When I let my feelings show,
My love starts to grow
Love is always growing inside,
Love is always growing inside
All I did was let my feelings show

When I let my anger go,
My joy starts to flow
When I let my anger go,
My joy starts to flow
Joy is always flowing inside,
Joy is always flowing inside
All I did was let my anger go

Repeat first verse

Words and music copyright 1981
by Living Love Publications,
Coos Bay, OR 97420

BE GENTLE WITH YOURSELF
By Haven

May you walk in laughter.
May you sing with joy.
May you build your home
In the warmth that you find.
There's the flow of love here.
Change of colors, too.
Waiting to surround us.
It's true.

Chorus

Be gentle with yourself.
Be gentle with yourself.
Be gentle with yourself.

May you feel your sorrow.
May you feel your pain.
May you find the answer
As your tears fall like rain.
Soon you'll find the suffering
Offers sweet release.
Then you'll be surrounded
In peace.

Chorus

And the gentleness reminds us
Of what we all can do.
May the love that it created
Be the light to see us through.

Chorus (Repeat 4 times.)

(In background: "In peace surround you
Or with peace surround you.")

I LOVE MYSELF THE WAY I AM
By Jai Michael Josefs

I love myself the way I am, there's
nothing I need to change.
I'll always be the perfect me, there's
nothing to rearrange.
I'm beautiful and capable of being the
best me I can,
And I love myself just the way I am.

I love you just the way you are,
there's nothing you need to do.
When I feel the love inside myself,
it's easy to love you.
Behind your fears, your rage and tears,
I see your shining star,
And I love you just the way you are.

I love the world just the way it is,
'cause I can clearly see
That all the things I judge are done
by people just like me.
So 'til the birth of peace on earth
that only love can bring
I'll help it grow by loving everything.

I love myself the way I am and still
I want to grow.
But change outside can only come
when deep inside I know.
I'm beautiful and capable of being
the best me I can,
And I love myself just the way I am.
I love myself just the way I am.

IT'S A BEAUTIFUL LIFE
By Tom Dalton

Chorus: It's a beautiful life that we live
        It's a beautiful life that we live

Wake up early
just to feel the morning sun
Greet the day with a song
Move your body to the rhythm
in your soul.
You can feel good today.

Chorus

Start the new day
with the dreams you have inside
You can reach them
if you keep your goals in mind
Don't you worry
if they seem so hard to find
You can feel good today.

Chorus

Try to live each day
as if it were the last
Show the love you feel
for everyone you pass
You can love your life,
just give it half a chance
You can feel good today.

Chorus

THANK YOU FOR MY LIFE
By Beth Towner Corwin (© 1981)

Thank you for my life
Thank you for my life
Each precious day is a gift to me
And I can hardly believe
the beauty I see.

Repeat

Thank you for my suffering
And the wholeness that it brings
Thank you for the trees in Spring
As they're budding and flowering.

Thank you for my frustration
My succumbing to temptation
For my growth and the lack thereof
That let me know I'm made of love.

Chorus

Thank you for my range of feelings
For the unexpected healings
For the process of growth
For love and hate
'cause I learn from both.

Thank you for the lessons unending
For the power of surrendering
For boredom and waiting to be free
Thank you for creating this for me.
Chorus

IT'S ALL ALL RIGHT
By Jai Michael Josefs

Whatever I'm feeling here and now
It's just what I'm feeling here and now
And it's all all right

Whatever I'm thinking here and now
It's just what I'm thinking here and now
And it's all all right

Whatever I'm doing here and now
It's just what I'm doing here and now
And it's all all right

Whatever I'm fighting here and now
It's just what I'm fighting here and now
And it's all all right

The secret's not in what I do
Or what I think or say to you
Or what I show or what I try to hide
The secret's not in what I feel
Or whether I'm making my dramas real
It's simply how much I accept
Whatever's going on inside

Wherever I'm angry here and now
It's just where I'm angry here and now
And it's all all right

Wherever I'm hurting here and now
It's just where I'm hurting here and now
And it's all all right

The secret's not in feeling good
Or living like I think I should
Or getting my desires satisfied
The secret's not in being strong
Or never doing anything wrong
It's simply how much I accept
Whatever's going on inside

La la la la la la la la
La la la la la la la la
And it's all right

Whatever I'm feeling here and now
It's just what I'm feeling here and now
And it's all all right
Yes it's all all right

LOOK FOR THE COMMON GROUND
By Tom Dalton

Living in a world of people,
how do we survive?
Living with so many people,
when will we realize
You and I, we're so alike. You and I,
we're so alike
And when I feel that I am right and
you are wrong
I just smile when I see your face
Remember there's a oneness space.
Try to see the world through your eyes
And even if our point of view
may seem to disagree
There's something we can understand,
I think that you'll agree.

Chorus:

We have to
Look for the common ground,
you can find it all around
Look for the love in everyone
Even if it's hard to see, you can find
the unity.
Just look for the love in everyone.

In our living day to day,
it's easy to forget
All our talk of brotherhood
just doesn't seem to fit.
There's a lot of broken hearts
with nothing left to believe
Now it's time we made a start,
it's up to you and me.

Chorus (twice)

. . . in everyone, everyone
(you and I we're so alike)
living in a world of people
(you and I we're so alike)
how can we survive
(you and I we're so alike)
living with so many people
(you and I we're so alike)
look for the common ground.

REMEMBERING AND FORGETTING
By Jai Michael Josefs

Sometimes I feel the spirit
Sometimes I feel so sad
Sometimes I feel so near it
Other times I hurt so bad
Some days it all feels wonderful
Some nights I want to cry
Sometimes I feel like my dreams can
   become real
And sometimes I just want to let them
   die

Chorus
Remembering and forgetting
That's the game that we play
We drift so far we forget who we really
   are
Until we remember that love is the way
To remember, to remember

The light that shines inside
Is brighter, brighter than the sun
But sometimes we ignore it
We're so busy try'n to get things done
Sometimes it all seems so important
What we say and how we do
And sometimes I feel the silence
And I know what's really true

Chorus

Sometimes illusions we create can seem
   so real
We lose sight of the love so easily
Sometimes we get so lost inside the pain
   we feel
Until we look around and see the learn'n
   to be free is just

Chorus

To remember
Remember (Repeat)